THE ULTIMATE GUIDE TO SPOKEN ENGLISH

SPOKEN ENGLISH MASTERY

BINOD DEY

ISBN 13:- 979-8885218580

First Print: December 4th, 2021
Revised Print: 2022

Published by Notion press
Notion Press, Inc.
800, West EI Camino Real #180,
California USA 94040
Notion Press Media Pvt Ltd,
#7, Red Cross Road,
Egmore, Chennai, Tamil Nadu 600008
Email ID: publish@notionpress.com
WEBSITE: https://notionpress.com/en

Dedicated to

my parents and all those who helped me to
turn this book into a success.

PREFACE

Hello learners,

This book is more than just a book. This is the book that will redefine you and connect you to yourself. It will guide you throughout your journey of learning English. This book is written in a simple and easy-to-understand language. Based on the author's knowledge of the language and communication skills, he has developed a unique way of presenting the English language.

Grammar is only one part of learning English. Listening, speaking, and developing communication skills are important skills as well.

This book presents everything from the basics, so you need no prior knowledge of English and Grammar to enjoy it. If you truly follow this book, you will become a native speaker.

Throughout this writing, the author has tried to use every method to make it more interesting for the reader. The book has been proofread and edited to the best.

About The Author

Binod Dey is a native Indian born in 2006. Currently, he is studying in a CBSE school in West Bengal for higher secondary education in the sciences. He is an International World Record Holder for "Youngest Author to write a book on Spoken English". His first published book is "Spoken English Mastery", which has now become one of the best-selling ebooks in the category of language learning and public speaking on Amazon. This has made him the world's youngest author to write a book on Spoken English. Learning English and communicating skills was something he did on his own. Therefore, he made up his mind to make others speak and he is now on the way to sharing his experiences, thoughts, ideas and the unique way to study grammar for fluency.

His first-ever book, 'Spoken English Mastery' was his first experience writing a book where he shared all his experiences and shared his knowledge to master English effortlessly.

ACKNOWLEDGEMENTS

Many people have played a crucial role in bringing up this book. It's an opportunity for me to express my gratitude to them.

Furthermore, I would like to thank Mr Sekhar Moitra for reading the manuscript and giving his valuable input. My sincerest thanks go to Ms Shubhangi Rajawat and Mr Rakesh Dey for their technical assistance.

I would like to thank my family for their patience and gracious support during the many long hours it took.

Binod Dey

TO THE LEARNERS

Below, I summarize the book that will help you extract the most value from it.
This book is divided into 3 parts.

Part A :- Basic English
Part B :- Basic Grammar
Part C :- Vocabulary and Pronunciation

Each part contains chapters that are essential.

Here are some tips that will help you follow the book.

1. Keep a pencil or highlighter nearby to highlight important points as you read.

2. To learn the correct pronunciation , meaning, and vocabulary of a word, use a pocket dictionary or search Google.

3. Use Google or YouTube for the reference of any topic in your regional language.

4. I recommend writing every topic with reference to your regional language if you are just learning this language.

CONTENTS OF THE BOOK

PART - 1 :- Basic English

Lessons

PART - 2 :- Basic Grammar

PART - 3 :- Pronunciation

PART - 1
BASIC ENGLISH

Lesson #1

The Alphabet

WHAT IS THE ALPHABET?

The Alphabet is a group of letters in English. The English Alphabet consists of 26 letters.

A	**B**	**C**	**D**	**E**	**F**
G	**H**	**I**	**J**	**K**	**L**
M	**N**	**O**	**P**	**Q**	**R**
S	**T**	**U**	**V**	**W**	**X**
		Y	**Z**		

The Alphabet is classified into two types :-

1. **Vowel** :- A, E, I, O, U
2. **Consonant** :- All the letters except the vowels are called Consonants.

Every little concept is the foundation for every big and tough concept. Hence, these little concepts need to be covered well.

Lesson #2

Formation of words and sentences

HOW ARE WORDS FORMED?

The letters in the Alphabet when combined form words.

eg :- Cat, Dog, Man etc.

Similarly, when words are combined in a proper form, they make sentences.

eg :- That man has a dog and a cat.

A Sentence is a group of words that are arranged in a proper form to make complete sense.

eg :- The sun rises in the east.
The cat is black.

PRACTICE EXERCISES

1. **Try making words from the letters of the alphabet.**
2. **Make three to four sentences for the following words.**

i) Cat	*iii) Boy*
ii) Car	*iv) Tiger*

Lesson #3

Days and Months

DAYS OF THE WEEK

There are 7 days in a week.

Each day of a week is written below with its correct pronunciation.

Days	Pronunciation
Sunday	*Sun - day*
Monday	*Mun - day*
Tuesday	*Tyuz - day*
Wednesday	*Wenz - day*
Thursday	*Thuz - day*
Friday	*Fraih - day*
Saturday	*Sah - tuh - day*

MONTHS OF A YEAR

There are 12 months in a year.

Each month of a year is written below with its correct pronunciation.

Months	Pronunciation
January	*Jah - nu - ary*
February	*Feb - ru - ary*
March	*March*
April	*A - pril*
May	*Mae*
June	*Joon*
July	*Ju - lai*
August	*Au - gusth*
September	*Sep - tem - buh*
October	*Ohk - to - buh*
November	*Nuh - vum - buh*
December	*Di - sem - buh*

Lesson #4

Greetings

Greetings play an important role in your life. They are very important in every language because they are referred to as conversation starters.
The first thing we do whenever we begin a conversation is to greet the other person or community.

The greeting we use is determined by the person we are speaking with.

Some important and daily use greeting phrases are given below :-

During Morning to 12 p.m.	***Good Morning***
During 12 p.m. to 4 p.m.	***Good Afternoon***
During 5 p.m. to 7 p.m.	***Good Evening***
During night	***Good Night***

Morning: maw - ning
Afternoon: aaf - tuh - noon
Evening: eev - ning
Night: nite

Formal Greetings (in office, school or any formal place)

- *Hello*
- *Good morning*
- *Good afternoon*
- *Good evening*
- *It's nice to meet you*
- *It's a pleasure to meet you*

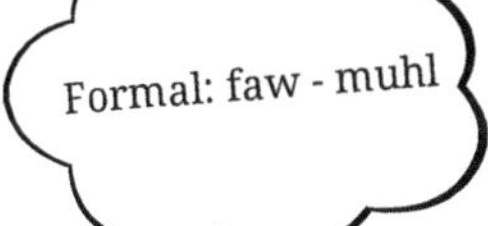

Informal Greetings (to family, friends etc.)

- *Hi*
- *Hey*
- *What's up*
- *Nice to meet you*
- *Pleased to meet you*
- *It's a pleasure*

WHAT AFTER GREETINGS?

Here are some phrases which you may use or you may be asked after greetings.

Formal ***(****in office, school or any formal place****)***

1. **It's nice to meet you or Pleased to meet you.**
   It's used for the person to whom you met for the first time.

2. **It's nice to meet you again.**
   It's used for the person to whom you met casually or you have already met before.

3. **How are you?**
   This is the most formal and common question which you may be asked after greetings. It is asked to know how you are?

Informal ***(****in office, school or any formal place****)***

4. **How's it going? or How are you doing?**
   This is the informal version of asking "how are you?"

5. **How are you? or How are things going on?**
   This is asked to know how have you passed your day.

Some common replies to some common questions which you may be asked during a conversation.

1. **How are you? or How are things going on?**

Reply:-
- Fine. How are things with you?
- I'm all right.
- Yeah, all right. (informal)
- *Way better than I deserve (informal)*

2. **What is your name?**

Reply:-
- My name is ___________.
- I'm ___________.

3. **Where are you from?**

Reply:-
- I'm from ___________.
- I belong to ___________.

4. **How old are you?**

Reply:-
- I'm 23 years old.
- I'm 23.

5. **What do you do**?

Reply:-
- I'm a student.
- I work in a post office.
- I'm unemployed at the moment.
- I work as a tour guide for a local tour company.

6. **What's your mobile number?**

Reply:-
- My phone number is xxxxxx6056.
- It's xxxxxx6056.

7. **What is your marital status?**

Reply:-
- I'm married.
- I'm single.

8. **Do you have any siblings** *(brother or sister)***?**

Reply:-
- I don't have any siblings.
- I have 2 brothers and 2 sisters.

Hobby means your favourite activity you like to do in your free time.

9. **What's your hobby** *(what do you like to do in your free time)***?**

Reply:-
- I like playing the guitar and reading books.
- My hobbies are playing the guitar and reading books.

10. **Do you have a** *(car/bike/pen)*?

Reply:-
- Yes, I have a (car/bike/pen).

11. **Can you speak English?**

Reply:-
- Yes, I can speak English very well.
- No, I am not able to speak English.
- I can understand English but I cannot speak English well.

12. **What's the weather like?**

Weather → veh·dhuh

Reply:-
- It's sunny.
- It's cloudy.
- It's raining outside.
- It's drizzling (Light rain)

12. **What time is it?**

Reply:-
- It's 10 o'clock.
- It's 10 a.m./p.m.

INTRODUCTION

A great introduction anywhere adds a great impression on your personality.

An introduction may be formal when we are at an interview or it may be informal when we are at a gathering or any occasion.

	FORMAL	INFORMAL
Greetings	• Good morning / afternoon / evening • Hello (sir/madam/ everyone)	• Good morning / afternoon / evening • Hello (sir/madam/ everyone)
Thanking (optional)	• Thank you for giving me this opportunity	—
Name	• I'm _________ • My name is ______	• I'm _________ • My name is ______
Place	• I'm from _______ • I belong to_______ • I'm from _____ but currently living in______	• I'm from _______ • I belong to_______ • I'm from _____ but currently living in______
Job	—	• I am a/an ______
Personality	• I am _______	—
Qualification	• I am in class ____ • I am in ______ • I have a master's degree in _____ from ______	• I am in class ____ • I am in ______ • I have a master's degree in _____ from ______
Skills/ Experience	• I'm a fresher • I have 3 years of experience in _____	—

	FORMAL	INFORMAL
Family (optional)	• There are ___(number) of us in my family	• There are ___(number) of us in my family
Hobby	• My hobbies are ______. • I like ______ • I'm interested in _____	• My hobbies are ______. • I like ______ • I'm interested in _____
Thanking	• That's about me. Thank you	• That's about me. Thank you

Example :-

- Hello sir,
- Thanks for giving me the opportunity.
- I'm Rakesh Jain.
- I'm from Udaipur but I'm living in Bengaluru.
- I'm a software engineer.
- I'm a creative and hardworking person.
- I have a masters degree in Computer science from Stanford University, California.
- I have 3 years of experience in this field.
- And also I am quite interested in singing.
- That's about me. Thank you.

Lesson #5
Manners

Manners play a very important role while you communicate.
Here are some phrases and words to use while communicating.

1. When you ask someone for something.
   - **Please**
   - **Kindly**
   - **May I have**

   eg:- *Please* give me that book.
   Could you *please* give me that pen?
   May I have a cup of coffee?

2. When you receive something from someone or when someone helps you.
   - **Thank you**
   - **Thank you so much**
   - **You are a lifesaver.**
   - **You rock.**

   eg:- *Thank you so much*, sir. (formal)
   You are a lifesaver, Sam. (informal)

3. When someone thanks you for something.
   - **You're welcome.**
   - **Welcome**
   - **Mention not**
   - **No problem**
   - **My pleasure**

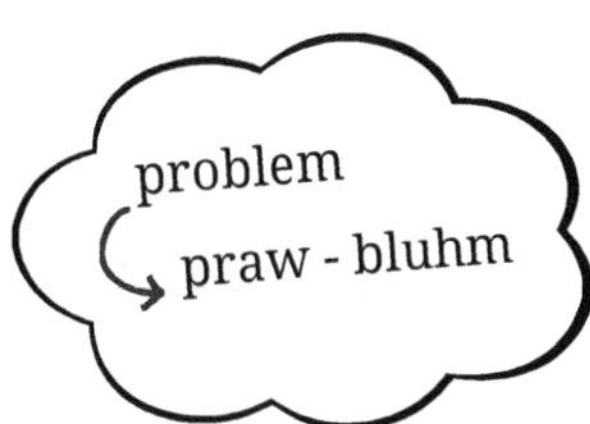

   eg:- *You're welcome*, Raman. (formal)
   My pleasure, Saroj (informal)

4. When you did not hear or understand what someone said to you.

- **I beg your pardon**
- **Pardon**
- **I'm sorry**
- **I didn't get it**
- **Excuse me**

eg:- ***Excuse me***, sir. Could you please repeat that?
I beg your pardon, sir.

5. When you wish to add something to the conversation

- **Sorry to interrupt you**
- **Sorry to intervene**

eg:- ***Sorry to interrupt you*** mam, but I think it's the best idea.

Lesson #6

Time

Time is the most important aspect of a person's life.
In this chapter, we will learn how to tell the time when someone asks, "What's the time?"

Let's begin by looking at the basics.

What time it is?

It is 3 o'clock.

What time it is?

It is 4:50 pm.

NOTE :-

1. a.m. is used to tell time in the morning.
2. p.m. is used to tell time in the afternoon.

PHRASES FOR TIME

1. Use 'a.m.' or 'p.m.'

3:15 in the afternoon :- It is 3:15 pm
9:10 in the morning :- It is 9:15 am.

2. When the minute hand is pointing from 1 to 30 minutes, use the following structure.

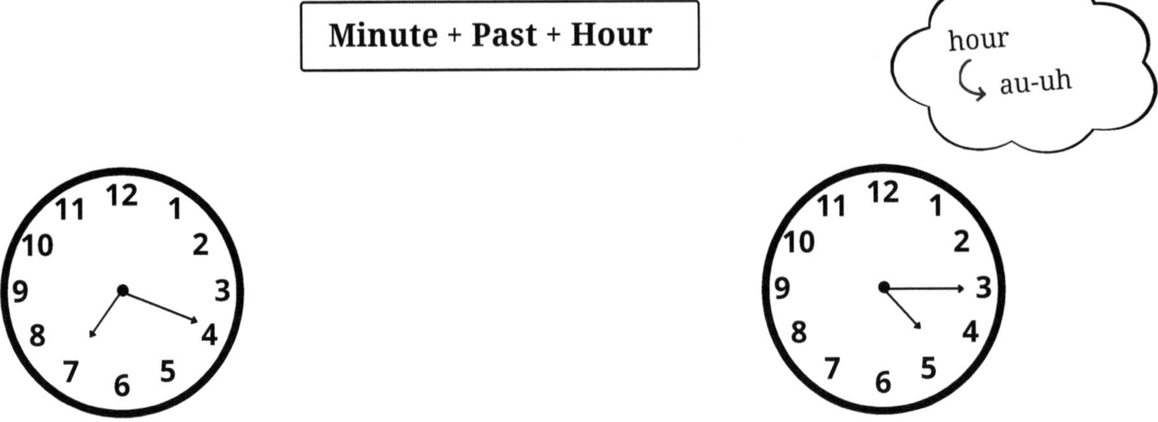

20 minutes past 7.

15 minutes past 5.

3. When the minute hand is pointing from 31 to 59 minutes, use the following structure.

Minutes left + To + Hour

10 minutes to 7.

20 minutes to 3.

4. Some special terms which are used to tell time

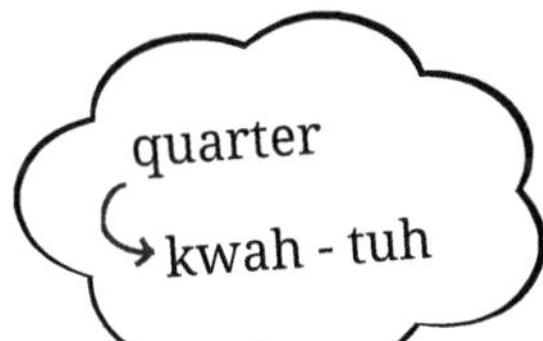

Quarter past :- It is used when the minute hand is at 15.

eg:- 3:15 = Quarter past 3
6:15 = Quarter past 6

Half past :- It is used when the minute hand is at 30.

eg:- 3:30 = Half past 3
6:30 = Half past 6

Quarter to :- It is used when the minute hand is at 45.

eg:- 3:45 = Quarter to 4
6:45 = Quarter to 7

Lesson #7

Numbers

Numbers are used in mathematics to count and label things.

CARDINAL NUMBERS

1	One	15	Fifteen
2	Two	16	Sixteen
3	Three	17	Seventeen
4	Four	18	Eighteen
5	Five	19	Nineteen
6	Six	20	Twenty
7	Seven	30	Thirty
8	Eight	40	Fourty
9	Nine	50	Fifty
10	Ten	60	Sixty
11	Eleven	70	Seventy
12	Twelve	80	Eighty
13	Thirteen	90	Ninety
14	Fourteen	100	Hundred

1000	One Thousand
10000	Ten Thousand
1,00,000	One Lac
1,00,00,000	One Crore

ORDINAL NUMBERS

Ordinal numbers are used to define the position of something

1st	First	15th	Fifteenth
2nd	Second	16th	Sixteenth
3rd	Third	17th	Seventeenth
4th	Fourth	18th	Eighteenth
5th	Fifth	19th	Nineteenth
6th	Sixth	20th	Twentieth
7th	Seventh	30th	Thirtieth
8th	Eighth	40th	Fortieth
9th	Ninth	50th	Fiftieth
10th	Tenth	60th	Sixtieth
11th	Eleventh	70th	Seventieth
12th	Twelfth	80th	Eightieth
13th	Thirteenth	90th	Ninetieth
14th	Fourteenth	100th	Hundredth

PART - 2
BASIC GRAMMAR

Lesson #8

The Sentences

A Sentence is a group of words that are arranged in a proper form to make complete sense.

In the previous chapters, we have learnt about the various letters in the English Alphabet and we saw how words were formed from those letters.
Now, let's see, how words can make sentences.

Sentences are of five types :-

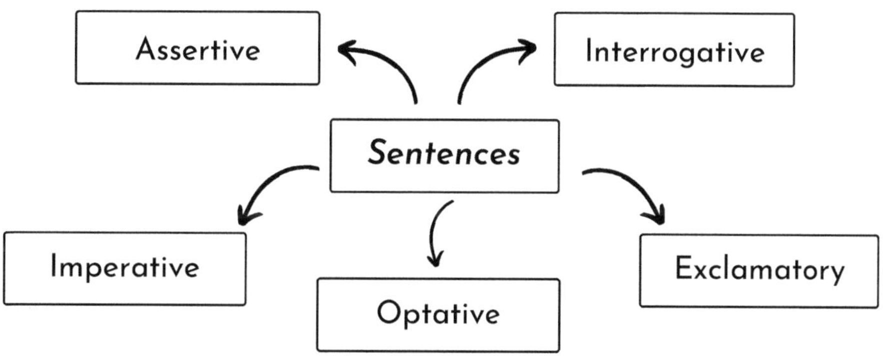

1. **Assertive Sentence**:- This type of sentence makes statements or states facts or ideas.
   eg:- Raju is learning English.

2. **Interrogative Sentence**:- This type of sentence asks questions.
   eg :- What is your name ?

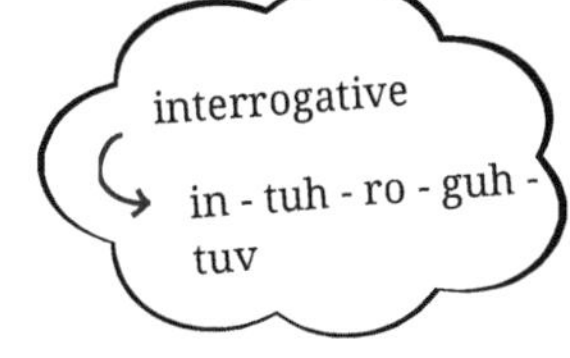

3. **Optative Sentence** :- This type of sentence expresses a prayer, wish, or curse.
   eg:- May God bless you.

3. **Imperative Sentence**:- This type of sentence expresses commands or requests.
   eg:- Shut the door.

4. **Exclamatory Sentence**:- This type of sentence expresses feelings.
   eg :- Wow! What a nice dress.

A Sentence is made up of three parts.

Sentence		
Subject	***Verb***	***Object***
• The Subject in a sentence is the name of a person or a thing which does the action or is being described. • Usually, it comes at the first in the sentence.	• The Verb in the sentence is the word which describes any action. • It denotes the action done by the subject. • Usually, it comes after the subject.	• The Object in the sentence is the word which is affected by the action done. • It may or may not be present in the sentence.

eg :-

Raju drives the car.

Here, Subject = Raju
Verb = Drives
Object = Car

He plays.

Here, Subject = He
Verb = Plays

SENTENCE STRUCTURE

To be called a sentence, a sentence must have a specific structure.
The structure of a normal and basic sentence is

Subject + Verb + Object

eg:- Gagan is drinking water.
(Subject) (Verb) (Object)

Sohan is playing.
(Subject) (Verb)

He and I are going to London tomorrow.
(Subject) (Verb) (Object)

Sanju is playing with a ball.
(Subject) (Verb) (Object)

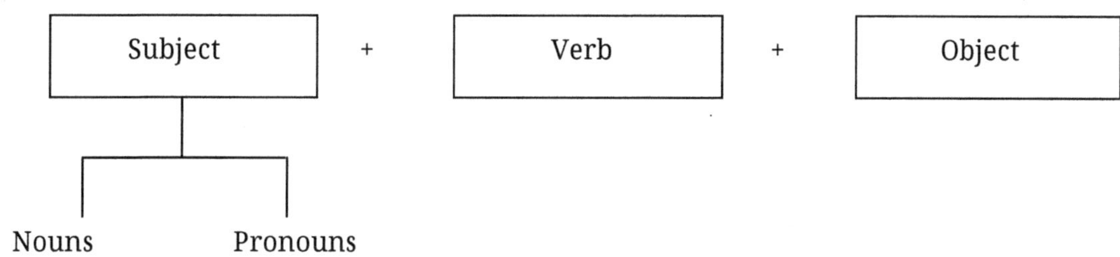

PRACTICE EXERCISE

1. **Identify Subject and verb in the sentence**

- He is playing cricket
- Mahesh is sleeping
- Samar goes to school.
- They are eating food.
- Aman is dancing.
- Radha is helping him with homework.
- Sunita plays the guitar.
- Jack is acting in the show.
- He works in the fields.
- Swimming is a good exercise.
- The cat is under the table.
- I jotted down her number on a scrap of paper.
- Do you know me?
- Vijaynagar is known for its greenery.
- Did Rama go to school?

2. **Rearrange the following jumbled words/phrases to make meaningful sentences.**

- lost / son / pen / his
- my family / with / I / to the park / went
- is / writing / Gopal / a letter / to her
- goes / there / Golu / often
- elders / respect / must / you / your
- like to / a book / I / read / sleeping / before
- he / to the school / does / go
- karishma / does not / he / know
- a white / pigeon / and / have / a black / I
- an apple / a doctor / away / a day / keeps

Lesson #9

Phrases and Clauses

We have already discussed what the sentence is.

However, some sentences do not make complete sense.

eg:- The baby is sleeping **in the room.**
He is driving **a blue car.**

The part of the sentences in the example that is highlighted that is **'in the room'** and **'a blue car',** do not make complete sense.

PHRASES

A phrase is a group of words without a subject or object. It makes sense but not complete sense.

eg:- a red car
in the room
in the east

CLAUSES

A clause is a group of words that form a part of a sentence and contain a subject and a verb.

eg:- Rahul laughs
She dances.
Suraj goes.

Lesson #10

Nouns

A Noun is a word used as the name of a person, place or thing.

eg:- ***Ashoka*** was a great emperor. (Ashoka is a name of a person.)
The ***pen*** is mine. (Pen is a name of a thing.)
Aman lives in ***India***. (Aman is a name of a person and India is the name of a country.)

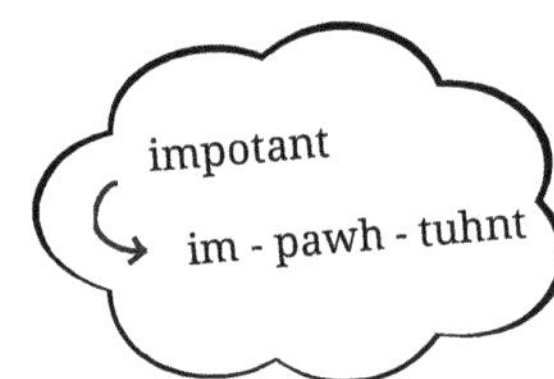

Why Nouns are important ?

Nouns act as the subject as well as the object in a sentence. As the subject is the most important part of the sentence, Noun also becomes important in a language.

Types of Noun

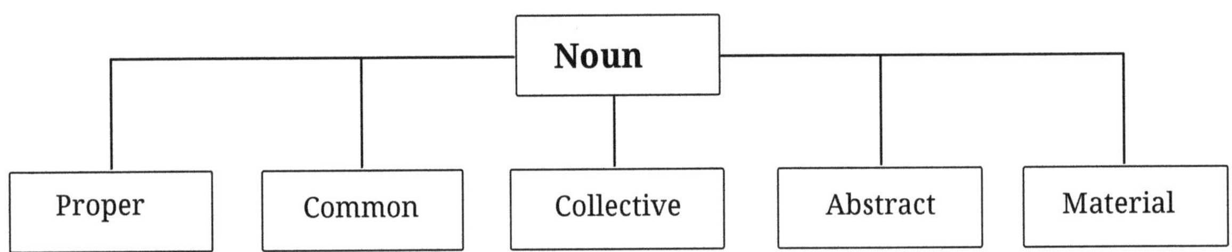

1. **Proper Noun** :- It is the name of a specific person, place or thing.
   eg :- Raju, Delhi, Taj Mahal , India, America, etc.

2. **Common Noun** :- It is the name given in common to every person, place or thing of the same kind.
   eg :-Car, city, boy, girl, school, king, etc.

3. **Collective Noun :-** It is the name of a collection of person or thing taken together as a whole.

eg :- An army = a collection of soldiers
A fleet = a collection of ships
A crowd = a collection of people, etc.

4. **Abstract Noun :-** It is the name of quality, action, emotion or state.

eg :- Quality = goodness, honesty, thickness
Action = laughter, hatred, theft
State = childhood, youth, sleep

5. **Material Noun :-** It refers to a material or substance from which things are made.

eg :- Gold, sugar, water, money, etc.

NOUN :- GENDER

Nouns can be classified as ***masculine*** or ***feminine*** or ***neuter*** (for things without life) based on Gender.

1. Masculine (male) :- boy, man, king, sir
2. Feminine (female) :- girl, woman, queen, madam
3. Neuter (non-living things) :- table, chair, book, car

FORMING MASCULINE AND FEMININE NOUNS

Masculine	***Feminine***
Boy	Girl
Brother	Sister
Father	Mother
Uncle	Aunt
Man	Woman
King	Queen
Bull	Cow
Horse	Mare
Sir	Madam
Son	Daughter
Nephew	Niece

Masculine	***Feminine***
Husband	Wife
Prince	Princess
Lion	Lioness
Host	Hostess
Actor	Actress
Waiter	Waitress
Hero	Heroine
Grandfather	Grandmother
Milkman	Milkwoman
Landlord	Landlady
Peacock	Peahen

NOUN :- NUMBER

The Noun further can be classified based on the number.
A noun that denotes only one thing is called ***Singular Noun.***
A noun that denotes more than one thing is called ***Plural Noun.***

Singular	*Plural*
Boy	Boys
Pen	Pens
Girl	Girls
Book	Books
Class	Classes
Brush	Brushes
Branch	Branches
Baby	Babies
Lady	Ladies
City	Cities
Story	Stories
Broom	Brooms
Army	Armies
Country	Countries
Chief	Chiefs
Proof	Proofs
Man	Men

Singular	*Plural*
Box	Boxes
Watch	Watches
Match	Matches
Mango	Mangoes
Buffalo	Buffaloes
Hero	Heroes
Photo	Photos
Thief	Thieves
Knife	Knives
Leaf	Leaves
Half	Halves
Woman	Women
Tooth	Teeth
Foot	Feet
Mouse	Mice
Child	Children
Ox	Oxen

Some nouns have singular and plural alike, such as sheep, fish, deer, series, species, pair, dozen, score

Some nouns are used only in plural, such as scissors, goggles, spectacles, trousers, jeans, pants, shorts, wages, savings, cattle, people

Some nouns look like plural but actually are singular, such as Mathematics, physics, ethics, politics, linguistics, athletics, news, etc.

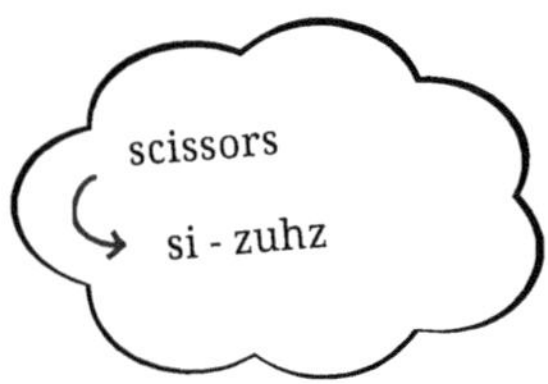

PRACTICE EXERCISE

1. **Think about the difference between Proper nouns and Common nouns.**

2. **Name the collective nouns for following.**

i) Collection of ants
ii) Collection of thieves
iii) Collection of players
iv) Group of bees
v) Collection of lions
vi) Collection of flowers
vii) Collection of sticks
viii) Collection ofsingers

3. **Rewrite the sentences by changing the gender.**

i) Ramesh gives the pen to him.
ii) All actors act well.
iii) The hen has found a worm.
iv) They have brought a new lion to the zoo.
v) My father went to the market with my sister.
vi) He is the host of the show.
vii) Sam played with my brother's cricket bat.
viii) You should ask him about his father's sickness.

4. **Underline the nouns and identify their types.**

i) Feel the breath, Sohan.
ii) Max is well-known for his juggling skills.
iii) The Peacock dances when it rains.
iv) They arrived here by train.
v) Sohan is getting himself ready for school.
vi) He laughs too much.
vii) Rahul is a sincere boy.
viii) The Pacific Ocean is very vast.
ix) Come, Tom, let's go for a walk.
x) At the playground, you get to observe a colony of ants.
xi) The scent of the perfume is delightful.
xii) The book is on the table.
xiii) Honesty is the best policy.
xiv) Sometimes it takes courage to tell the truth.
xv) His family live in different countries.

5. Rewrite the sentences by changing the number of nouns.

i) I have got a pen in my box.
ii) Mohan has many sheep on his farm.
iii) The driver gets the car washed.
iv) Tanisha has a different passport.
v) Samir is a teacher and he teaches kids in his town.
vi) Who is hiding behind the bush?
vii) I love to play with the ball.
viii) Where are my scissors?
ix) She had a pair of white shoes when she was a kid.
x) How can you make a sweater out of that wool?

3. Correct the erros in the following sentences.

i) He has many friend in his school.
ii) We are coming to America in the next three day.
iii) Samaira has a pair of shoes while I have a scissors.
iv) Dogs shouts at me.
v) Sheeps bleat while dogs bark.
vi) The officers had their gun on their shoulder.
vii) Amir is the boy who keeps her table clean.
viii) She has a lot of works.

Lesson #11
Pronouns

A Pronoun is a word used instead of a noun.

Compare the following sentences.

Deepak is ill. Deepak should visit a doctor.

Deepak is ill. **He** should visit a doctor.

In the second sentence, the word "Deepak" is replaced with "He". Therefore, "He" is a pronoun.

Types of Pronouns

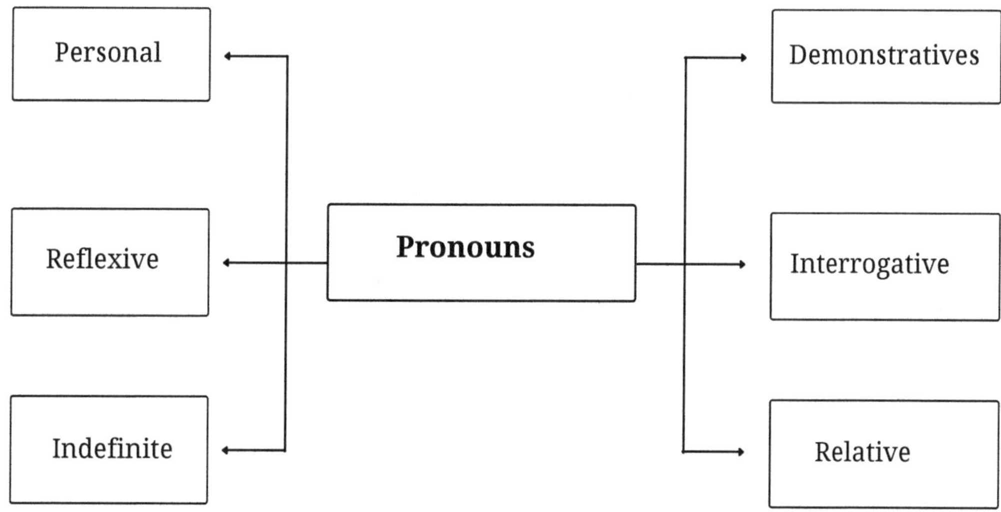

PERSONAL PRONOUNS

I, we, you, he, she, it, they are called ***personal pronouns.***
There are 3 persons in personal pronouns.

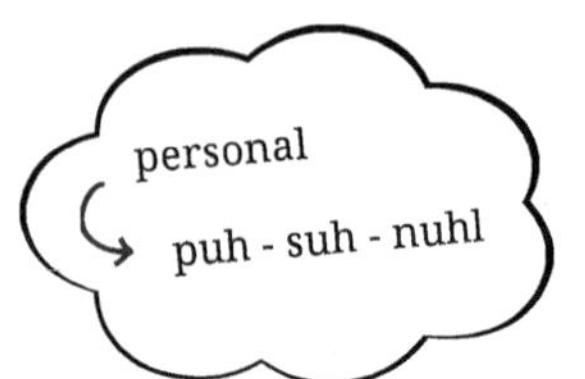

First person :- *the person speaking.*
Second person :- *the person spoken to.*
Third person :- *the person spoken of.*

The pronouns discussed above are categorized on the basis of persons.

Persons	Personal Pronouns	Examples
First Person	I We	***I*** am reading. ***We*** are reading.
Second Person	You	***You*** are reading.
Third Person	He (male) She (female) It (neuter) They	***He*** is reading. ***She*** is reading. ***It*** is reading. ***They*** are reading.

There are 3 cases for personal pronouns.

1. **Subjective case**
2. **Objective case**
3. **Possessive case**

1. **Subjective case :-** When a pronoun is used as a subject in a sentence, it is called the sentence, it is called the ***subjective case of a personal pronoun***.
   eg:- I am reading a book. (Here "I" is used as a subject.)

2. **Objective case :-** When a pronoun is used as an object in a sentence, it is called the ***objective case of the personal pronoun.***

eg:- Rahul is playing with me. (Here, "Me" is used as an object.)

3. **Possessive case :-** When a pronoun is used to show ownership or possession in a sentence, it is called the ***possessive case of the personal pronoun.***

eg:- This is my cycle. (Here, "My" is used to show ownership.)

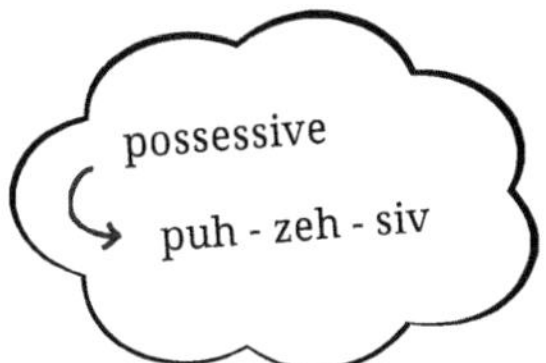

Here is a list of every personal pronoun with their cases.

Persons	**Subjective case**	**Objective case**	**Possessive case**
First person	I We	Me Us	My / Mine Our
Second person	You	You	Your
Third person	He She It They	Him Her It Them	His Her Its Their

Examples of the subjective case of the personal pronoun.

I am reading a book.
He is listening to music.

Examples of the objective case of the personal pronoun.

Garima plays with *me*.
Let's play with *him*.

Examples of the possessive case of the personal pronoun.

This is *my* ball.
She has *her* dress.

REFLEXIVE PRONOUN

When -self is added to my, your, him, her, it and -selves to our, your, them, we get what are called Compound Personal Pronouns.

My	Myself	Our	Ourselves
Your	Yourself	Them	Themselves
Him	Himself		
Her	Herself		
It	Itself		

These pronouns are called ***Reflexive Pronouns*** when the action done by the subject reflects upon the subject.

eg:- I hurt ***myself***.
He would hurt ***himself***.
You would hurt ***yourself***.
We would hurt ***ourselves***.

RELATIVE PRONOUNS

A Relative Pronoun is a pronoun that relates the subject with the current incident.
The Relative pronouns used in English are:-

i) **Who** = used with person

eg:- This is the man ***who*** came here yesterday.
That is the boy, ***who*** is the most intelligent in our class.

ii) **Which** = used with non-living things and animals

eg:- The monkey ***which*** is sitting on the branch jumps higher.
The pen ***which*** you got yesterday was mine

iii) **What** = used to express thoughts, things

eg:- I know ***what*** he wants to say.
I mean ***what*** I say.

iv) **That** = used to speak about a specific person, animal or thing.

eg:- He is the boy ***that*** can help you.
A city ***that*** is built on rivers

v) **Whom** = used to speak about a person in objective case.

eg:- He is the boy ***whom*** I play with.
This is the man to ***whom*** I gave my pen.

vi) **Whose** = used to speak about a person, place or thing in possessive case.

eg:- The boy ***whose*** shoes are white is the leader.
This is the question ***whose*** solution is not known to anyone.

vii) **When** = used to speak about a time when the incident took place.

eg:- I came here *when* you went to the hospital.
They were playing ***when*** I was asleep.

viii) **Where** = used to refer to the place where the incident occurred.

eg:- He wanted the address of the place where yesterday.
My friend lives in the building where you went.

INDEFINITE PRONOUNS

An indefinite pronoun is a pronoun that refers to a person or a thing without being specific.
The Indefinite pronouns used in English are:-

i) **Anyone** = an additional or different thing.

eg:- I want ***another*** ice cream.

ii) **Anybody** = any person

eg:- Does ***anybody*** have watercolours?

iii) **Each** = every person seen separately.

eg:- ***Each*** student will bring ten rupees tomorrow.

iv) **Either** = one or the other of two people

eg:- *Either* he or my brother is guilty.

v) **Neither** = not one and not the other. (none of the two things or persons)

eg:- ***Neither*** Tom nor Bill was present.

vii) **Enough** = as many as needed.

eg:- I have eaten ***enough*** sweets for now.

viii) **Other** = a different person or thing from the one already mentioned.

eg:- She wants the ***other*** dress.

ix) **Someone** = an unknown person.

eg:- ***Someone*** is trying to reach me.

x) **Both** = two people or things.

eg:- Raman wants ***both*** the toys.

xi) **Several** = more than two but not many.

eg:- I have been to Taj Mahal ***several*** times.

xii) **All** = whole quantity of something.

eg:- ***All*** animals on earth are not harmful.

xiii) **None** = not any quantity.

eg:- There are ***none*** toffees left in the jar.

PRACTICE EXERCISE

1. Identify the Pronoun in the sentence

- Raja is a boy.
- He is the tallest boy in the class.
- I wanted to meet him on his birthday.
- It is their cow.
- That information was confidential between Raj and me.
- What did you think would happen when you did that?
- Somebody must have seen the driver leave.
- Shall we follow his instructions or theirs?
- The dog bit itself.
- She and her friend came over.

2. Complete the sentence by choosing correct pronouns.

- Have you told _____the good news? (she, her)
- Mom drove _____ to school today. (I, me, my)
- She cannot come with _____ today. (We, us, our)
- _____ mom always told me to believe in myself. (I, me, my)
- Don't touch _____ (my, mine) phone.
- I don't want to share _____ (we, our, ours) work with the other team because it's ______ (we, our, ours).
- After the parade, _________ met up in the town square. (something, anywhere, everyone)
- John likes to do things by ________. (myself, himself, themselves)
- Everyone ate early. When we arrived, ________ was left. (that, such, none)
- They bought new furniture for ________ house. (mine, their, ours)
- ________ am learning to speak better English. (I, he, me)
- __________ must not praise oneself. (some, one, any)
- __________ is the meaning of fragrance? (who, what, which)
- We aren't sure __________ got here first. (why, who, whom)
- This is the boy __________ Igave my ball. (who, whom, whose)

3. Complete the sentence by filling the gaps with correct pronouns.

- They have hurt _____
- I will wash my clothes__________
- The man _____ is honest is trusted.
- The ball ______ Raman got in the park yesterday was mine.
- This is the car _____ belongs to my uncle.
- Ranjana is the girl ______ gets good grades and she is the one ________ I taught economics.
- The man ____ does not work hard will not get results.
- The boy ________ I met yesterday was the leader of the cricket team.
- I came here __________ you were asleep.
- Mr Samar lives in the building _______ you went to yesterday.
- Jindal Sharma is the one ________ knows Mr Motilal very well.
- She wants ______ ice cream.
- _________ Kris ____ you have stolen my pencil box

Lesson #12

Verbs

***Verbs** are words that describe actions, whether physical or mental. Verbs also describe a "state of being."*

eg:- Radha *dances*.
Krishan is *singing* a song.
My watch is *damaged*.
The glass is *brittle*.

verbs → vuhbz

TYPES OF VERBS

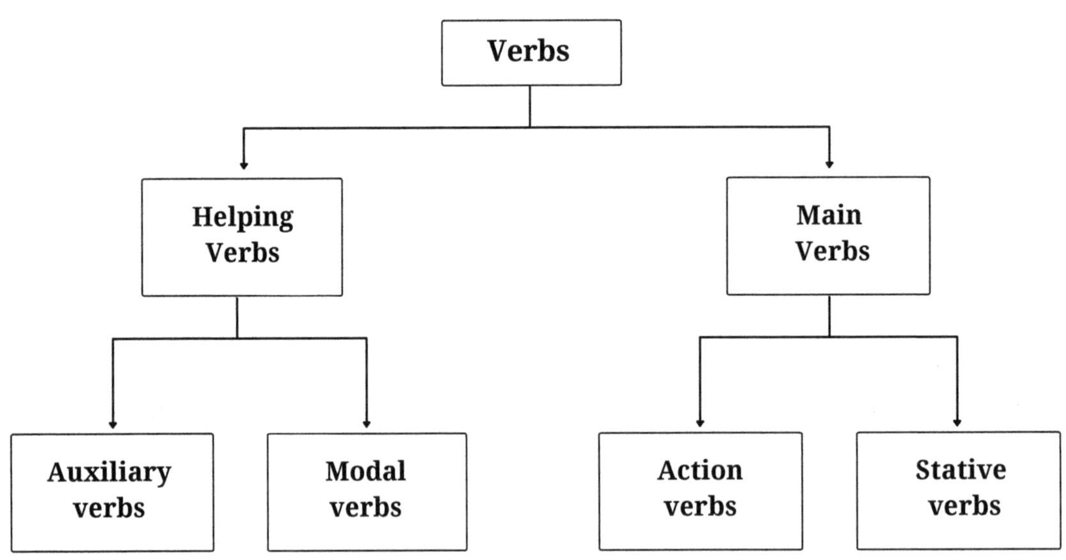

HELPING VERBS

Helping verbs are, as the name suggests, verbs that help another verb. They provide support and add additional meaning.
It helps the main verb to denote whether the action happened in past, or is happening in the present, or is going to happen in the future.

eg:- Ravi *is* playing. ("Is" denotes that the action is happening at present.)
The dog *was* barking at me. ("Was" denotes that the action happened in past.)
I *will* go to the library in the evening. ("Will" denotes that the action will take place in the future.)

Helping verbs are of two types:-

1. **Auxiliary verbs**
2. **Modal verbs**

1. **Auxiliary verbs:-** These are helping verbs that describe the tense of the main verb. This is the most important part of any sentence.

   The important auxiliary verbs are:- ***be, have, and do.***
   These verbs have different forms which are used according to their need.

2. **Modal verbs:-** These verbs are used to express permission, possibility, certainty, and necessity.

   Some modal verbs are:- ***can, may, could, would, will, etc.***

The auxiliary verbs with their different forms and uses are given below:-

Auxiliary verbs	**Forms**	**Use**	**Examples**
Be (Continuous)	*Is*	singular	He is playing.
	Am	with "I"	I am playing
	Are	plural + you	We are playing.
	Was	singular	He was playing.
	Were	plural + you	We were playing.
Have (Perfect)	*Has*	singular	He has played.
	Have	plural + I + You	They have played.
	Had	with every subject	I had played.
Do (Simple)	*Do*	plural + I + You	We do play ourselves.
	Does	singular	Does he go there?
	Did	with every subject	Did he go there?

The chapter on TENSES will provide a detailed look at AUXILIARY VERBS.

MAIN VERBS

Main verbs are the words that describe the action performed by the subject.

Main verbs are of two types:-

1. **Action verbs**
2. **Stative verbs**

1. **Action verbs:-** The verbs that describe physical or mental actions are called Action verbs.

   eg:- eat, talk, walk, sleep, run, read, etc. (Physical actions)
   guess, grow, live, succeed, fail, etc. (Mental actions)

2. **Stative verbs:-** The verbs that describe the state, feelings of the subject are called Stative verbs.

   eg:- want, love, hate, feel, taste, see, hear, etc.

Forms of Main verbs

Main verbs (except stative verbs) have four forms of verbs.
There are **four forms of verbs:-**

1. ***First form (Root form) :-*** This form is the root form of the main verbs.
2. ***Second form (Past form) :-*** This form is the past form of the root verb.
3. ***Third form (Past participle form):-*** This form of the verb partakes the nature of both verbs and adjectives.
4. ***Fourth form (Present participle):-*** This form of the verb is similar to the third form but it has the suffix **-ing** with the root verb.

Some important verb forms are given below

V1	V2	V3	V4
Accept	Accepted	Accepted	Accepting
Achieve	Achieved	Achieved	Achieving
Add	Added	Added	Adding
Adopt	Adopted	Adopted	Adopting
Advise	Advised	Advised	Advising
Agree	Agreed	Agreed	-
Allow	Allowed	Allowed	Allowing
Arrive	Arrived	Arrived	Arriving
Ask	Asked	Asked	Asking
Bake	Baked	Baked	Baking
Beat	Beaten	Beaten	Beating
Become	Became	Become	Becoming
Behave	Behaved	Behaved	Behaving
Bend	Bent	Bent	Bending
Boil	Boiled	Boiled	Boiling
Bring	Brought	Brought	Bringing
Build	Built	Built	Building
Burn	Burnt	Burnt	Burning
Buy	Bought	Bought	Buying
Call	Called	Called	Calling
Catch	Caught	Caught	Catching
Change	Changed	Changed	Changing
Chase	Chased	Chased	Chasing
Chew	Chewed	Chewed	Chewing
Clap	Clapped	Clapped	Clapping
Come	**Came**	**Come**	Coming
Cry	Cried	Cried	Crying
Damage	Damaged	Damaged	Damaging
Dance	Danced	Danced	Dancing
Dream	Dreamed / dreamt	Dreamed / dreamt	Dreaming
Earn	Earned	Earned	Earning
Enjoy	Enjoyed	Enjoyed	Enjoying
Feel	Felt	Felt	Feeling
Fight	Fought	Fought	Fighting
Find	Found	Found	Finding
Fry	Fried	Fried	Frying
Get	Got	Got	Getting
Hate	Hated	Hated	-
Hang	Hung/hanged	Hung/hanged	Hanging
Have	Had	Had	
Hold	Held	Held	Holding
Introduce	Introduced	Introduced	Introducing

V1	V2	V3	V4
Joke	Joked	Joked	Joking
Jump	Jumped	Jumped	Jumping
Keep	Kept	Kept	Keeping
Kick	Kicked	Kicked	Kicking
Kill	Killed	Killed	Killing
Laugh	Laughed	Laughed	Laughing
Lay	Laid	Laid	Laying
Learn	Learned	Learned	Learning
Leave	Left	Left	Leaving
Lie	Lied	Lied	Lying
Listen	Listened	Listened	Listening
Make	Made	Made	Making
Marry	Married	Married	Marring
Meet	Met	Met	Meeting
Move	Moved	Moved	Moving
Offer	Offered	Offered	Offering
Open	Opened	Opened	Opening
Paint	Painted	Painted	Painting
Pay	Paid	Paid	Paying
Print	Printed	Printed	Printing
Punish	Punished	Punished	Punishing
Purchase	Purchased	Purchased	Purchasing
Relax	Relaxed	Relaxed	Relaxing
Run	Ran	Run	Running
Say	Said	Said	Saying
Sell	Sold	Sold	Selling
Send	Sent	Sent	Sending
Sit	Sat	Sat	Sitting
Sleep	Slept	Slept	Sleeping
Smell	Smelt	Smelt	-
Spell	Spelt	Spelt	Spelling
Stand	Stood	Stood	Standing
Sweep	Swept	Swept	Sweeping
Talk	Talked	Talked	Talking
Teach	Taught	Taught	Teaching
Tell	Told	Told	Telling
Use	Used	Used	Using
Visit	Visited	Visited	Visiting
Win	Won	Won	Winning
Want	Wanted	Wanted	-

V1	V2	V3	V4
Begin	Began	Begun	Beginning
Bite	Bit	Bitten	Biting
Blow	Blew	Blown	Blowing
Break	Broke	Broken	Breaking
Choose	Chose	Chosen	Chosing
Do	Did	Done	Doing
Drink	Drank	Drunk	Drinking
Drive	Drove	Driven	Driving
Eat	Ate	Eaten	Eating
Fall	Fell	Fallen	Falling
Fly	Flew	Flown	Flowing
Forget	Forgot	Forgotten	Forgetting
Give	Gave	Given	Giving
Go	Went	Gone	Going
Grow	Grew	Grew	Growing
Hide	Hid	Hidden	Hiding
Ride	Rode	Ridden	Riding
Ring	Rang	Rung	Ringing
See	Saw	Seen	-
Shake	Shook	Shaken	Shaking
Sing	Sang	Sung	Singing
Sink	Sank	Sunk	Sinking
Swim	Swam	Swum	Swimming
Wake	Woke	Woken	Waking
Wear	Wore	Worn	Wearing

SOME VERBS WITH SIMILAR FORMS			
Cost	Cost	Cost	Costing
Cut	Cut	Cut	Cutting
Hit	Hit	Hit	Hitting
Hurt	Hurt	Hurt	Hurting
Put	Put	Put	Putting
Read	Read	Read	Reading

PRACTICE EXERCISE

1. Underline the main verb and circle the helping verb in each sentence.

- I am studying the wonderful life of Tim, the dog.
- My class will write reports about this sports tournament.
- We have read an exciting account of her triumphs.
- Jensie is painting a picture of the royal Bengal tiger.
- Max and I are working on a poster about Rama's victories.
- Wilma had overcome serious physical problems.
- Her mother had given her a great deal of support.
- The people in Wilma's hometown were cheering for her.
- People will remember his accomplishments for many years.
- Her story has inspired young athletes around the world.

2. Fill in the blanks with correct Helping verbs.

- We _________ practised tennis in the indoor games room.
- Ravi _________ writing his diary.
- Sushila _________ come tomorrow.
- She _________ ill today.
- They _________ my friends.
- Samir _________ the tallest boy in our group.
- We _________ not talk to strangers.
- _________ you play here?

3. Choose the correct verb in each sentence.

- We __________ (has paid/have paid) him the money.
- She ________ (want/wants) to go.
- My brother ________ (enjoy/enjoys) playing cricket.
- The teacher _________ (teach, taught) the lesson yesterday.
- He _________ (is waiting, are waiting) for the results.
- Yesterday, I __________ (received, was received) her reply.
- By the time I'm 50, I _______ (will make, will have made) a million dollars.
- She _______ (lives, lived, living) here before she moved to Cambridge.
- I will _______ (spent, spends, spend) all the money I take with me.
- We ________ (meet, met, will meet) here yesterday.
- We ________ (has thought, had thought, will have thought) the test was going to be easy.
- I'm thinking about _________ (take, taking, takes) some time off work.

Lesson #13

Adjectives

An <u>Adjective</u> describes or modifies nouns and pronouns in a sentence. It normally indicates quality, size, shape, duration, feelings, contents, and more about a noun or pronoun.

Adjectives usually provide relevant information about the nouns/pronouns they modify/describe by answering the questions: What kind? How many? Which one? How much?

eg:- He is an ***honest*** man. (Of what kind ?)
There are ***no*** pictures in the book. (how much ?)
I want ***that*** balloon. (which one ?)
I ate ***some*** rice. (how much ?)

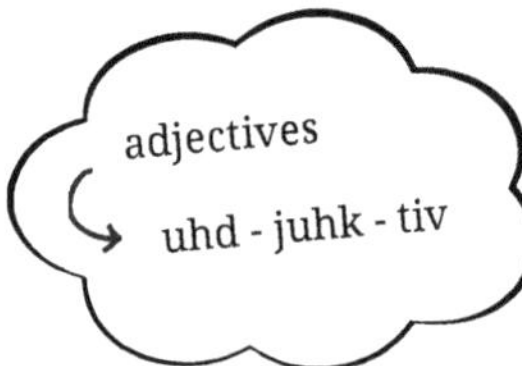

Read the following sentences and identify the adjectives.

1. Tasha is a ***sincere*** student.
2. It is a ***broken*** toy.
3. ***Many*** kites are flying in the sky.
4. Aman wants ***that*** car.
5. I have been to Surat ***many*** times with my parents.

TYPES OF ADJECTIVES

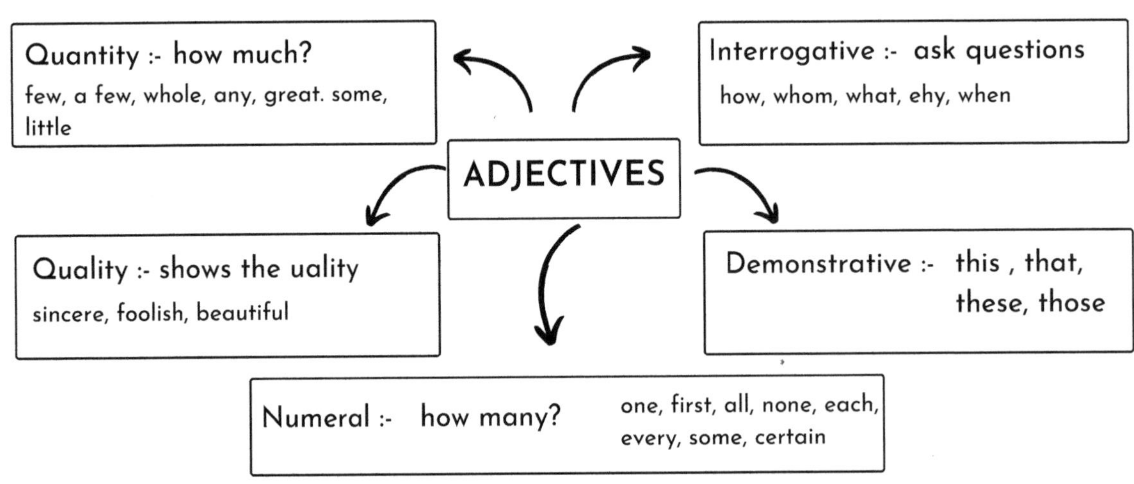

COMPARISON OF ADJECTIVES

Read the following sentences.

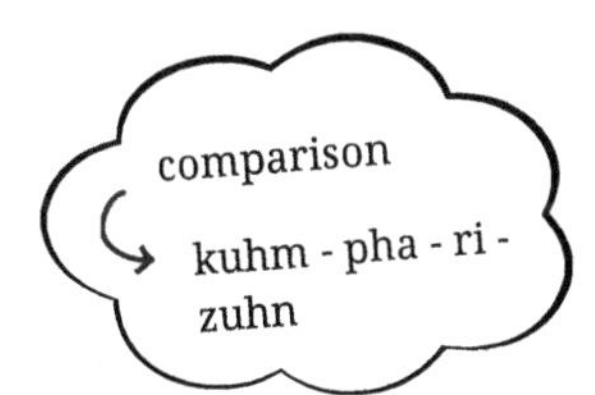

Sam is *wise*.
Ram is *wiser* than Sam.
Hari is the *wisest* of all.

In sentence 1, the adjective "**wise**" tells us that Sam is wise without saying how wise he is.
In sentence 2, the adjective "**wiser**" tells us that Ram is wiser when both Ram and Sam are compared.
In sentence 3, the adjective "**wisest**" tells us that Hari is the wisest person when compared with every person in the room.

The adjective "*wise*" is said to be in the ***Positive degree.***
The adjective "*wiser*" is said to be in the ***Comparative degree.***
The adjective "*wisest*" is said to be in the ***Superlative degree.***

*The **Comparative degree** denotes a higher degree of quality when two things are compared.
The **Superlative degree** denotes the highest degree of quality when more than two things are compared.*

Here are some common adjectives used in daily life with their degree of comparison

Positive	Comparative	Superlative
Sweet	Sweeter	Sweetest
Small	Smaller	Smallest
Tall	Taller	Tallest
Young	Younger	Youngest
Fast	Faster	Fastest
Sharp	Sharper	Sharpest
Slow	Slower	Slowest
Weak	Weaker	Weakest

Positive	Comparative	Superlative
Brave Close Cute Dense Fine Large Pure Rare Safe	Braver Closer Cuter Denser Finer Larger Purer Rarer Safer	Bravest Closest Cutest Densest Finest Largest Purest Rarest Safest

Positive	Comparative	Superlative
Happy Easy Heavy Wealthy	Happier Easier Heavier Wealthier	Happiest Easiest Heaviest Wealthiest

Positive	Comparative	Superlative
Fat Thin Big Hot Sad	Fatter Thinner Bigger Hotter Sadder	Fattest Thinnest Biggest Hottest Saddest

Positive	Comparative	Superlative
Beautiful Intelligent Difficult Delicious	More Beautiful More Intelligent More Difficult More Delicious	Most Beautiful Most Intelligent Most Difficult Most Delicious

Positive	Comparative	Superlative
Good	Better	Best
Bad	Worse	Worst
Little	Less	Least
Many	More	Most
Old	Elder, Older	Eldest, oldest
Far	Farther	farthest
Late	Later, latter	latest, last
In	Inner	innermost, inmost
Out	Outer	Outermost, utmost

The dual form of the comparative and superlative degree of the adjectives given above are used in different ways.

1. ***Later, latter ; latest last***

- Later and latest refer to time.
- Latter and last refer to position.

eg:- We are ***later*** than him.
The ***latter*** chapter is difficult than this chapter.

2. Elder, older ; eldest, oldest

- Elder and eldest are used for persons and members in the same family.
- Older and oldest are used for both persons and animals.

eg:- John is elder than Jack. (John and jack are of the same family)
John is older than Jack. (John and jack are not of the same family)

Some example sentences for Comparative degree.

- Rachit is *wiser* than his elder brother.
- Sam is ***more intelligent*** than Kapil.
- The second part of the film is ***more interesting*** than the first one.
- Mt. Everest is ***taller*** than Mt. Fuji.
- A car is ***smaller*** than an aeroplane.

Some example sentences for Superlative degree.

- He is the ***smartest*** boy in the class.
- Mt. Everest is the ***highest*** mountain in the world.
- This is the ***best*** book I have ever read.
- Suman is the ***most beautiful*** girl in the class.
- The Statue of Unity is the ***tallest*** statue in the world.

PRACTICE EXERCISE

1. Identify the adjectives in the sentences.

- He is a man of few words.
- The gentleman standing there is a very loyal friend of my dad.
- I like Italian food.
- I ate some rice with freshly prepared tomato soup.
- He has only five kites.
- Ramu was once a cunning thief.
- In fairy tales, some hungry giants eat people.
- Football is fast and exciting.
- Sports are beneficial and fun.
- The food tasted bitter.

2. Choose the correct adjective for the following sentences.

- I am _______ (smart, smarter, smartest) than him.
- Sushil is the _________ (good, better, best) bowler in our team.
- Kaushali is looking __________ (beautiful, more beautiful)
- He is the __________ (wise, wiser, wisest) of all.
- Aman is my __________ (older, elder) brother.
- There are __________ (no, none) pictures in this book.
- I ate _______ (all, much, some) rice.
- Sohan is an _________ (good, honest, wise) man.
- Maria is my __________ (eldest, oldest, old) daughter.
- He made no __________ (further, farther, far) complaints.
- This is the __________ (nearest, next, near) post office to my house.
- The bride was much __________ (young, younger, youngest) than the groom.
- The offer was too ___________ (good, better, best) to be true.
- He is much ___________ (good, better, best) now.
- The ________ (great, first, one) prize was won by Sarvesh.
- The ship sustained __________ (heavy, heavier, heaviest) damage.

3. Fill in the blanks with correct forms of the adjectives.

- The majority accepted the _________ (later, latter) proposal.
- I have an _________ (elder, older) sister.
- Raman is _________ (elder, older) than Suresh.
- I cannot run any _________. (farther, further)
- Join my channel to get the _________ (latest, last) information.
- Annie is the _________ (intelligent, most intelligent) girl in the class.
- He knows how to sell things at the _________ (good, best) prices.
- This is the _________ (bad, worst) idea that I have come across.
- This is the _________ (nearest, next) police station to my house.
- The _________ (latest, last) time I saw him, he was in his high spirits.

4. Fill in the blanks with correct forms of the adjectives.

Raju:- Hey, Ravi.
Ravi:- Hello Raju. How are you?
Raju:- I am _________. How is your brother today? Is he _________? {Good}
Ravi:- Yes, he is well now. The doctor has told my brother to take the medications properly.
Raju:- Which doctor have you been to?
Ravi:- I have been to Dr.Mathur.
Raju:- Oh, yes. He is one of the _________ doctors in the city. {Good}

Lesson #14
Adverbs

An Adverb is a word that describes a verb, an adjective or another adverb. Adverbs answer the questions like when, where, how, how much, how often, etc.

eg:- She looks ***really*** beautiful. (how)
They will stay ***here tonight***. (where, when)
He is ***too*** careless. (how much)

TYPES OF ADVERB

Adverbs are of 5 types.

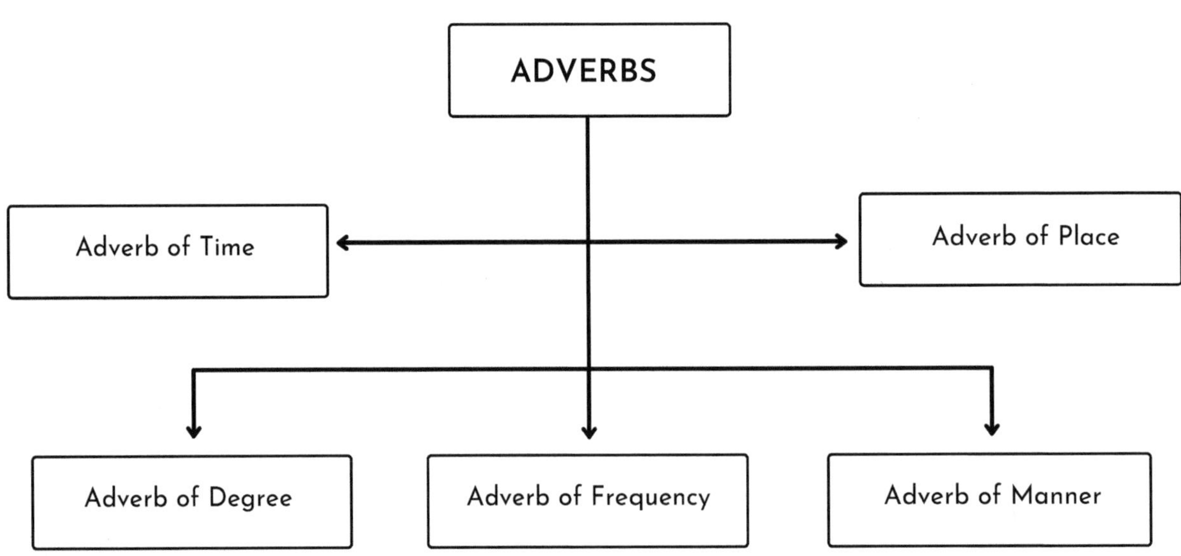

1. **Adverbs of Time**

- It answers the question of "when".
- Some adverbs of time are:- soon, later, before, daily, today, yesterday, tomorrow, never

eg:- I have seen this movie ***before***.
Sam played football ***yesterday***.
She practices the violin ***daily***.

2. **Adverbs of Place**

- It answers the question of "where".
- Some adverbs of place are:- here, there, up, down, in, out.

eg:- Ram has gone ***there***.
Amit looked ***up***.
She walked ***out***.

3. **Adverbs of Degree**

- It answers the question of "how much" or "to what extent".
- Some adverbs of degree are:- too, very, little, almost, nearly, enough, quite.

eg:- My brother is **very** intelligent.
Fatima is ***quite*** busy with her work.
I have ***almost*** finished my homework.

4. **Adverbs of Frequency**

- It answers the question of "how often".
- Some adverbs of frequency are:- once, twice, thrice, never, often, frequently, again

eg:- Zeeshan called me ***twice***.
She ***often*** visits the library.
I have been to the Taj Mahal ***once***.

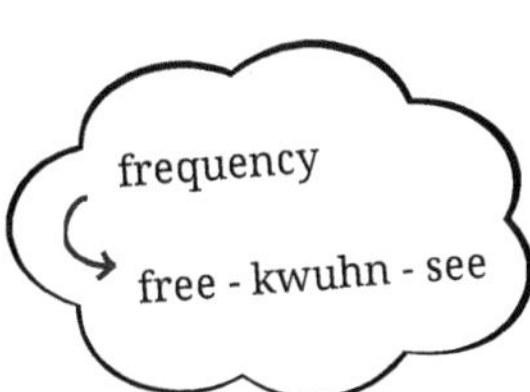

5. **Adverbs of Manner**

- It answers the question of "how"
- Some adverbs of manner are:- fast, clearly, really, hard, bravely, slowly.

eg:- He runs ***fast***.
Chirag reads ***clearly***.
Suman writes ***slowly***.

PRACTICE EXERCISE

1. Choose the correct adverb

- He comes here ________. (daily. several, twice)
- The Sikhs fought ________. (brave, bravely, very)
- I can bowl ________. (fast, fastly, daily)
- I ________ (usually, ever, once) go to bed at 10p.m.
- He has ________ (ever, never, none) been to U.S.A.
- My grandparents live in Kerala. I visit them ________. (once, often, several)
- She ________ (often, frequently, twicw) cleans her room.
- Are you ________ (very, fast, quite) sure?
- We started the journey________. (early, quite, frequently)
- The bus ________ (daily, always, often) arrives at 4 p.m.

2. Underline the adverbs in the following sentences.

- The boy is too careless.
- The winds are very strong.
- The baby slept soundly.
- The soldiers fought the war valiantly.
- Joey always tries his best.
- Surely you are mistaken.
- The movie is to end soon.
- Your friend messaged again.
- I did my homework already.
- I was rather busy.
- Is your mother within?
- We looked for the lost puppy everywhere.
- We do not know her.
- How long is the trip?
- Monica seldom visits here.

3. Put the adverbs at correct places in the following sentences.

- I go to school. {always}
- He comes late. {generally}
- Action Fighter is my favourite show, and I watch it on Saturday. {every}
- I forget to do the homework. {Sometimes}
- Someone is calling me. {frequently}
- We go to a movie theatre. {occasionally}
- She is standing. {outside}
- Ramlal has kites on his roof. {many}
- Ask him if he knows where does Rama go? {usually}

Lesson #15

Conjunctions

A Conjunction is a word that joins two words, phrases (group of words that don't make a complete sentence) or clauses (a normal sentence with a subject and a verb).

eg:- and, but, or, as if, as soon as, than, etc.

Read the following sentences.

eg:- I ate rice and dal for the lunch.
He is smarter than I am.
Rajiv and Satish are good batters.
Either take it or leave it.

TYPES OF CONJUNCTIONS

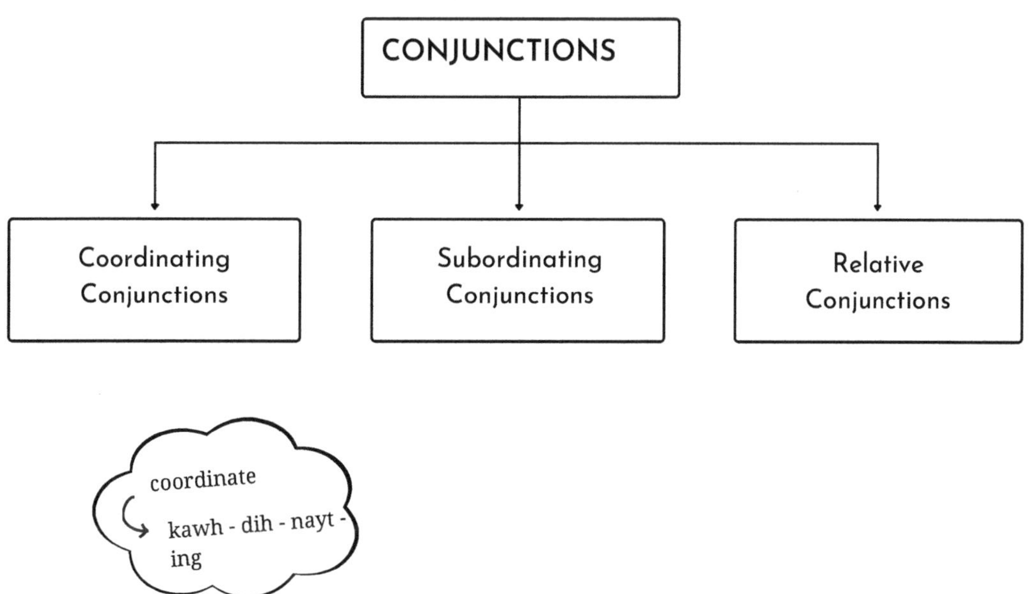

1. Coordinating Conjunction

It connects two words, phrases or clauses that are grammatically equal

They always come between the words or phrases or clauses they join.

These conjunctions can be remembered through an acronym, ***FANBOYS*** :-

Conjunctions		***Use***	***Examples***
F	**For**	*because or since*	I have to buy a new car, for I have sold the old one.
A	**And**	*in addition to*	Ramesh and Sneha are my friends.
N	**Nor**	*and not*	She didn't talk to me, nor did she call her friends.
B	**But**	*however*	I want to go but I am busy with my work.
O	**Or**	*either (choice)*	Give me a burger or a pizza
Y	**Yet**	*but*	He does hard work, yet he didn't pass the exam.
S	**So**	*therefore*	She was busy with her class, so she could not play.

2. Subordinating Conjunction

It joins a dependent clause (no meaning of its own) to an independent clause (has the meaning of its own).

They can come in between or can come earlier in a sentence.

The conjunctions in this category are:- ***after, as, because, before, till, by the time, as soon as, when, only if, if, that, etc.***

eg:- I have my class ***after*** breakfast.
He has a cold ***because*** he ate an ice cream yesterday.
I will leave ***as soon as*** the train arrives.
You will pass ***if*** you work hard.

3. Correlative Conjunction

It joins two words, phrases or clauses that carry equal importance in a sentence.

They mostly work in pairs

The conjunctions in this category are:- ***either...or, neither...nor, not only...but also, both...and, though...yet, whether...or***

eg:- I would buy ***either*** chocolate ***or*** ice cream. (choice)
Neither he ***nor*** I am wrong. (no one)
I am ***not only*** a teacher ***but also*** a motivational speaker.

PRACTICE EXERCISE

1. **Choose the correct conjunctions for the following sentence**

- This is the place _______ we stayed last time we visited. (where, when, how)
- You won't pass the test _______ you study. (when, if, unless)
- I could not get a seat, _______ I came early. (as, though, when)
- _______ had I taken my shoes off _______ I found out we had to leave again. (no sooner / than, rather / than, whether / or)
- My car has a radio _______ a CD player. (but, or, and)
- Raja _______ Sohan are brothers. (or, and, if)
- He works hard _______ he doesn't get the results. (yet, because, or)
- He ran away_______ he was afraid. (but, because, nor)
- Is this book mine _______ yours? (nor. such, or)
- _______ You or I am mistaken. (neither, though, either)
- You could leave _______ you are not well. (if, then, from)
- The train arrived _______ he arrived at the station. (though, as soon as, then)
- I was annoyed ,_______ I kept quiet. (yet, still, and)
- _______ he was not there, I spoke to his brother. (for, as, after)
- Two _______ two makes four. (and, or, so)

1. **Fill in the blanks with the the correct conjunctions .**

- I missed the bus _______ I was late for college.
- He is poor _______ he is proud.
- He is rich _______ he is kind.
- You _______ I are friends.
- _______ take it _______ leave it.
- I do not care whether you go _______ stay.
- Naresh didn't talk to me _______ did he blame me for the robbery.
- We shall stay in the hotel _______ you return.
- He tried _______ he didn't succeed.
- Two _______ two make four.
- He lost his balance _______ fell off his bicycle.
- It is a long time _______we last saw him.
- He will be there _______ he leaves the office.
- I will definitely buy that shoes _______ I will go back.
- He is better at drawing _______ me.
- Did he just graduate? I don't believe _______ he seems to be too young.
- _______ he is there, I shall visit him the next morning.

Lesson #16
Prepositions

Prepositions are used to express the relationship of a noun or pronoun (or another grammatical element functioning as a noun) to the rest of the sentence.

eg:- in, on, for, to, of, with, and, about, beside, behind, etc.

He is playing ***under*** shade.
I am going ***with*** Mohan.
She is going ***to*** a party

Prepositions can be broadly divided into eight categories: time, place, direction or movement, agency, instrument or device, reason or purpose, connection, and origin.

Category	Prepositions
Place	at, in, on, by/near/close to, next to/beside, between, in front of, behind, above/over, below/under
Time	at, in, on, during, for, since, by, until, before, after
Direction	to, from, over, under, along, around, across, through, into, out of, toward(s), etc.
Origin	from, of
Reason	for, through, because of, on account of, from
Connection	by, with

PREPOSITIONS OF PLACE

Prepositions	Uses	Examples
At	specific points or locations	He is going to stay ***at*** G-86 in Sector 26.
In	enclosed spaces	The biscuits are ***in*** the container.
On	surfaces or tops of things	The cat is sitting **on** the table.
Near, close to	lack of distance	He lives ***near*** my house.
Next to, beside	adjacency	I was standing ***beside*** Mr. Sharma.
Behind	something at the back of something.	Samar was hiding ***behind*** the door.
Between	something in the middle of two person or things.	He put the veggies ***between*** the sandwiches.
In front of	something situated before something	I cannot recognize the boy who was standing i***n front of*** me.
Above, over	to show something higher	A beautiful bird flied **over** me.
Below, under	to show something lower	The ball was kept ***under*** the table.
Among	something kept between many things.	I was the only Hindi speaker ***among*** the crowd.

PREPOSITIONS OF TIME

Prepositions	Uses	Examples
At	specific and short times of day	Let's meet ***at*** noon.
In	months, years	I was born ***in*** August 1995.
On	days and dates	The meeting is organised ***on*** 23rd March.
For	duration of time	Aman studied ***for*** many hours.
Since	to indicate an event which began at a specific point of time in the past	He has been watching television ***since*** 2 p.m.
By	a specific point in the future before which an event must be completed	Raman and Mahesh would complete the project ***by*** Saturday.
Until	a continuous event that will terminate at a specific point in the future	They would continue to protest ***until*** their demands are fulfilled.

PREPOSITIONS OF MOVEMENT / DIRECTION

Prepositions	Uses	Examples
To	movement with a specific aim or destination.	They went **to** Kolkata the last year.
From	movement with a specific point of origin	We will return **from** America the next week.
Along	movement on a straight line	We walk **along** the road everyday.
Around	movement in circular direction	The kids were moving **around** me for chocolates
Across	movement from one end to other end	The train moved **across** the tunnel.
Through	movement from one end to other end in an enclosed space.	The thief entered the jewellery showroom **through** the window in the washroom.
Towards	movement closer to something	He is going **towards** the library.
Onto	movement ending on something	The cat jumped **onto** the table.
Into	movement ending inside something.	The boy jumped **into** the swimming pool.
Off	movement away from something	Put **off** your shoes, Ajay.

PRACTICE EXERCISE

1. Identify the Preposition in the following sentences.

- He is going to Mumbai by train.
- Sheetal lives in an H-78 apartment.
- Why don't you come along with me?
- Vishakha is moving towards the green corridor.
- He was born in Mohali but stays in Hyderabad.
- I have eaten nothing since yesterday morning.
- A bird flew over the coconut tree.
- He is superior to me.
- I was astonished at his success.
- Who is knocking at the door?

2. Choose the correct Preposition for the following sentences.

- He gets up _____ 7 a.m. (at, in, on)
- Jayesh was hiding _____ the almirah. (from, behind,off)
- Thomas was coming _____ Delhi _____ Dubai. (to, off ; near, from)
- They got married _____ August 23. (on, in, at)
- There is a ball ______ that chair. (off, under, into)
- We went _______ the stairs. (through, down, into)
- He has been writing _____ two hours.
- Wasir loves to walk _____ the river. (across, along, through)
- You are the only brilliant student _________ (in, among, across)
- She has been reading __________ (since, for, at) 9 a.m.

3. Fill in the blanks with appropriate prepositions.

- Pour some milk _________ my cup.
- Cows feed _________ grass.
- He died _________ his country.
- The moon does not shine _________ its own light.
- They drove _________ Mumbai _________ Allahbad _________ car.
- Everyone laughed _________ him.
- He is junior _________ me _________ service.
- He has been charged _________ theft.
- The Rajdhani Express will arrive _________ 4 p.m.
- _________ rice they had curry.
- The bees were flying _________ my head.
- The driver jumped _________ the car.
- The crew fell short _________ food.
- David jumped _________ the river.

Lesson #17
Interjections

Interjections are words that are independent of the surrounding words. It has no meaning of its own but expresses a strong feeling.

eg:- Oh!, Hurray!, Wow!, Alas!, Bravo! etc.

Read these sentences:-

i) ***Hurray!*** we won the match
ii) ***Hey!*** What are you doing there?
iii) ***Alas!*** He is no more.
iv) ***Bravo!*** You did a great job.

Some common interjections are:-

Joy	Hurray!, Wow!,
Grief	Alas!, Ouch!
Surprise	What!, Oh!, Ha!
Approval	Bravo!, Well done!, Great!
Attention	Listen!, Look!, Behold!, Hush!
Greeting	Hey!, Hi!, Hello!

Lesson #18

Articles

Articles are words that define a noun as specific or unspecific.
The words a, an or the are called Articles.

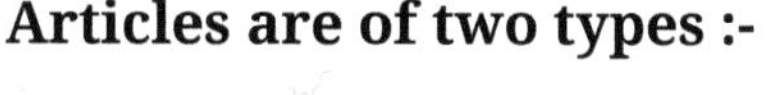

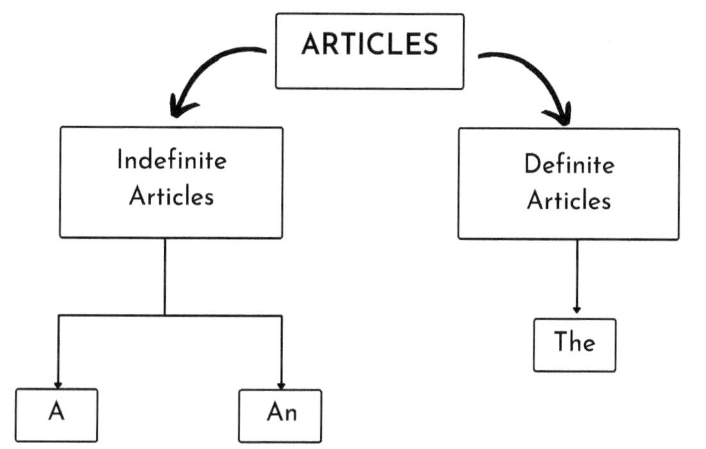

INDEFINITE ARTICLES

- A or An are called Indefinite articles.
- The word a or an used in English to refer to a person or thing that is not identified or specified.
- The choice between A or An is determined by the sound of the letter by which the word is starting.
- A is used before a consonant letter sound of a letter by which the word starts.
  eg:- A cup of tea. (any cup of tea)
  An apple (any apple)
- An is used before a vowel sound of the letter by which the word starts.
  eg:- An ice cream (means any ice cream)
  An orange (means any orange.)

- Some words which may start with a consonant have a vowel sound. Such terms require "An" before they are used.

  eg:- An honest boy. (here, h is silent, therefore it is pronounced as "onest")
  An hour

- Similarly, some words which may start with a vowel letter, have consonant sounds. Such words use "A" before they are used.

  eg:- A University.

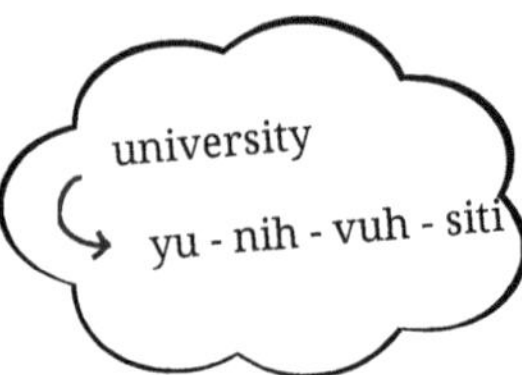

DEFINITE ARTICLES

- "The" is referred to as a Definite article.
- The is used before some proper nouns (names)
  - a) names of oceans and seas {The Pacific, The Arabian sea}
  - b) names of rivers {The Ganga, The Yamuna}
  - c) names of mountain ranges {The Himalayas}
  - d) names of unique things of their kind {The sun, The earth}

OMISSION OF ARTICLES

There are some cases where the articles are not used.

- Before names of uncountable nouns.

  eg:- ***Gold*** is a shiny metal. (not "The Gold")

- Before most Proper nouns { names of people, continents, countries, cities, mountains }

  eg:- ***Raja*** lives in ***India***. (not "The Raja" or "The India")

- Before names of meals.

  eg:- ***Lunch*** is ready. (not "The Lunch")

- Before names of languages.

  eg:- I learn ***English***. (not "The English")

- Before names of relations, like father, mother, brother, sister, etc.

  eg:- ***Father*** returned home. (not "The Father")

REPETITION OF ARTICLES

The Articles if or if not repeated, changes the meaning of the sentence.

eg :- If I say, "She has *a* black and white dress."
It means, she has a dress which is black and white in colour.

If I say, "She has *a* black and *a* white dress."
It means, she has two dresses, one black in colour and another white in colour.

Now compare these sentences.

1. The manager and coach is absent.
2. The manager and the coach are present.

In the first sentence, it refers that the manager and the coach are both same person. It means the single person is both manager and coach.

In the second sentence, it refers that the manager and the coach are both different people. It means there are two persons, one is the manager and another is the coach.

PRACTICE EXERCISE

1. Use the correct articles in the following sentences.

- He is not ____ honest man.
- Radha has ____ beautiful dress.
- ____ sun shines brightly.
- English is ____ easy language.
- We wait for him ____ hour.
- She is ____ untidy girl.
- Rahul has wasted _____ hour.
- Nile is ____ largest river in the world.
- He has got his admission in ____ university.
- Coffee is cultivated as ____ beverage.
- I want ____ best quality.
- ____ sun rises in ____ east.
- Akbar was ____ third emperor
- You should visit ____ doctor.
- He was ___ first man to pass the test.

2. Explain if the sentences given below are correct with reference to the use of articles.

- He is the European.
- Do you like butter?
- Art is the wonderful subject.
- I want to drive car.
- She eats the apple every day.
- I need a water.
- Who is the man?
- Radha has got new mobile phone, but its not an android phone.
- Should I take admission into an university or a college after completing my high school?
- All the committed members have arrived at on decision.

Lesson #19

Apostrophe

An apostrophe is a small punctuation mark (') placed after a noun to show that the noun owns something.

apostrophe
uh - paws - truh - phee

USES OF APOSTROPHE

1. **to show *possession.***

- Use an apostrophe +"s" ***('s)*** to show that one person/thing owns or is a member of something.

  eg :- Amir's ball. (Ball of Amir)
  Radha's dress. (Dress of Radha)
  Kanak's house. (House of Kanak)

- If a plural noun ends with "s", do not add 's at the last, instead add only " ***Apostrophe*** " to the plural noun.

  eg :- The boys' club. (The club of boys)
  The animals' jungle. (The jungle of the animal)

- If a plural noun does not ends with "s", add an apostrophe +"s" ('s)

  eg :- The children's class. (The class of children)
  The men's dress showroom. (The dress showroom of men)

2. **to indicate that, letters have been removed to form a contraction**

- When you combine two words to make a contraction, you will always take out some letters. In their place, you add an apostrophe.

  eg :- They will = They'll
  He would = He'd

Important Contractions		
Is	's	It's , She's , He's (It is , She is ....)
Am	'm	I'm (I am)
Are	're	We're , They're (We are , They are)
Have	've	We've , They've (We have ....)
Has	's	It's , She's , He's (It has , She has ....)
Had	'd	I'd , He'd , We'd (I had, He had .....)
Would	'd	They'd , She'd (They would....)
Will	'll	He'll , I'll , We'll (He will , I will)

PRACTICE EXERCISE

1. Use apostrophe to transform the following sentences.

- The ball of Ramesh.
- The house of Garima.
- The responsibility of the Government.
- I am reading the book of Akhilesh.
- He is the son of my uncle.
- Let us play, Akshay.
- He is here, Jack.
- Who is standing there?
- Do not make noise.
- You should not disobey your elders.

2. Select the correct word from the choices

- The team lost (its/it's) the first game of checkers.
- Air Force (33s/33's) mission is to rescue stranded sea turtles.
- Lakshya borrowed (James'/Jamses/James's) book.
- My quilt is in the small room while the (other's/others'/others's) quilts are in the big room.
- (You're/your) not allowed to do that.
- (Who's/Whose) going to the game with us?
- My grades are all (As/A's).
- Mona's (parent's/parents') house is in Sikkim. They love it there

Lesson #20

Demonstratives

A Demonstrative is used to point to something specific within a sentence. These can indicate items in space or time, and they can be either singular or plural.

There are total four demonstratives.

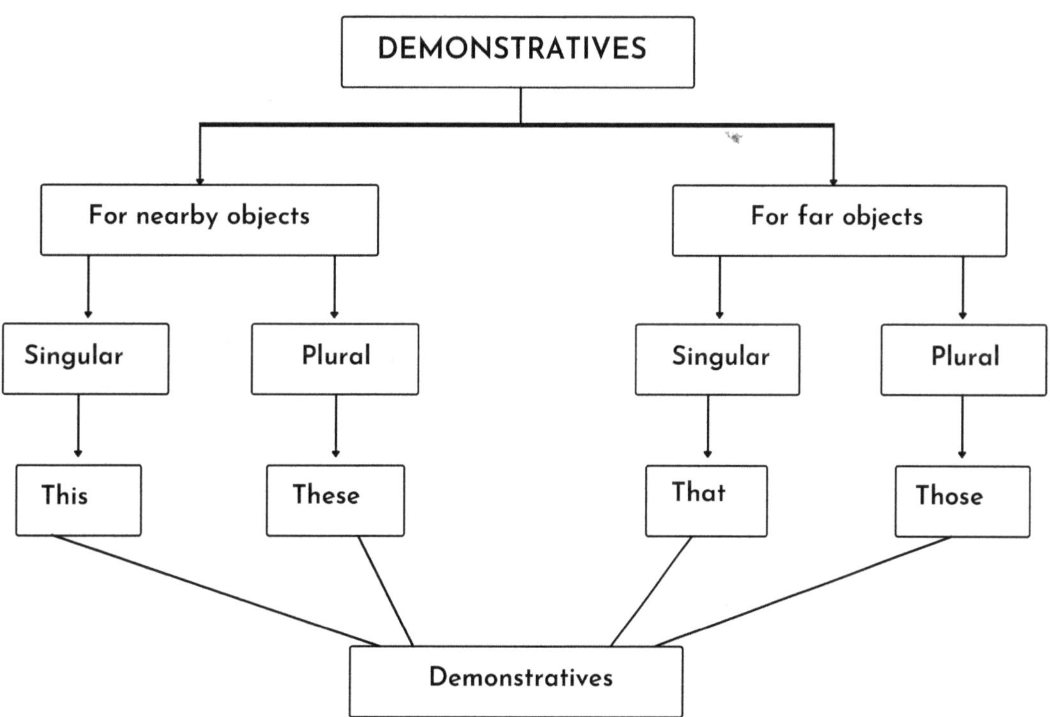

- ***"This"*** is used to refer singular noun which is close at hand. Similarly, "***These"*** is used to refer to plural nouns close at hand.

eg:- *This* is my book.
These are my books.

- ***"That"*** is used to refer singular noun which is far at hand. Similarly, ***"Those"*** is used to refer to plural nouns far at hand.

eg:- ***That*** is my pen.
Those are my friends.

- "***That"*** and ***"Those"*** are also used to avoid the repetition of preceding nouns.

eg:- My shirt is better than ***that*** of him. (It means " My shirt is better than his shirt."
Our work is much easier than ***those*** of other classes.. (It means "Our work is much easier than the work of other
classes."

PRACTICE EXERCISE

1. Look around yourself. You will see many objects around you. Use correct Demonstratives to point out the objects you see.

Lesson #21

Quantifiers

Quantifiers are words or groups of words, which are used before a noun to show the amount or quantity of that noun.

To have a better understanding of this topic, let's revisit nouns. Nouns are categorised into two types based on quantity.

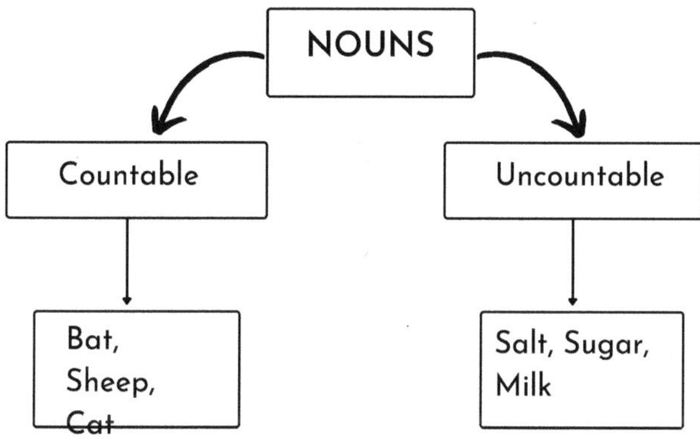

with countable nouns	with uncountable nouns	with both
Many Few / A few Several A large number of	Much Little / A little A bit of A large quantity of	More Less Some Lots of All, Enough None

Examples :-

i) There is ***a little*** money left in my wallet.
ii) There is ***a little*** milk left in the can.
iii) Here are **some** tomatoes in the basket.
iv) There are ***several*** books which you need to check out.

Here are some Quantifiers with their correct usage :-

i) **Some** = used with sentences with a positive meaning. Also used in questions which expect 'yes' in reply.

eg:- I have **some** tomatoes in the basket.
Can you give me **some** toffees?

ii) **Any** = used with sentences with a negative meaning. Used majorly in interrogative sentences. Also used in questions to which you do not expect any reply.

eg:- I don't have ***any*** money.
Do you have ***any*** dresses for me?

iii) **Little / Few** = means 'not much' i.e., in a negative sense.

eg:- I have ***little*** water. (nearly no water left)
I know ***few*** of your friends.

iv) **A little / A few** = means 'some though not much' i.e., in a positive sense.

eg:- I have ***a little*** water. (there is some water)
I still have ***a few*** kites left.

v) **The little / The few** = means 'not much but all there is' i.e., in a positive sense.

eg:- I wasted ***the little*** water I had. (there is sufficient water)
He burnt ***the few*** books he had.

PRACTICE EXERCISE

1. **Choose the correct quantifiers.**

- There are ______ (some, little, much) tomatoes left in the basket.
- Are there ______ (some, any, few) mangoes on the tree?
- There is ______ (a little, a few, many) water in the bucket.
- _______ (little, few, several) knowledge is a dangerous thing.
- I have _______ (a little, few, many) money in my wallet.
- He knows _________ (little, a little, the little) English. It is enough for him.
- Bill didn't drink all the water. There's _______ (any, little, a little) water left.
- There isn't _________ (some, any, few) furnitures at home.
- This is a very boring place to live. There's _________ (little, few, some) to do.

2. **Fill in the blanks with appropriate quantifiers.**

- It seems we have had ____________ assignments in English this year.
- There aren't very ____________ books in the library.
- It has rained very ____________ this summer, that's why the grass is so brown.
- John had ____________ money with him so he couldn't even buy a bus ticket.
- There is not very ____________ dancing going on at the party.
- He is an introvert, therefore he has got ____________ friends.
- Have you visited ____________ foreign countries?
- Although he's very ill, he didn't take ____________ medicine.
- Are there ____________ apples on the tree?
- Only ____________ friends came to visit him.
- There are ____________ tomatoes left. I don't think it's ____________ to make tomato ketchup.
- The ____________ money I had was stolen by a thief in the crowd.
- There is ____________ traffic today.
- Don't eat so ____________ cake.

Lesson #22

WH Family

WH Family is a group of words that are used to form questions (interrogative sentences)
These words are :- What, why, when, who, whom, whose, which, how, etc.

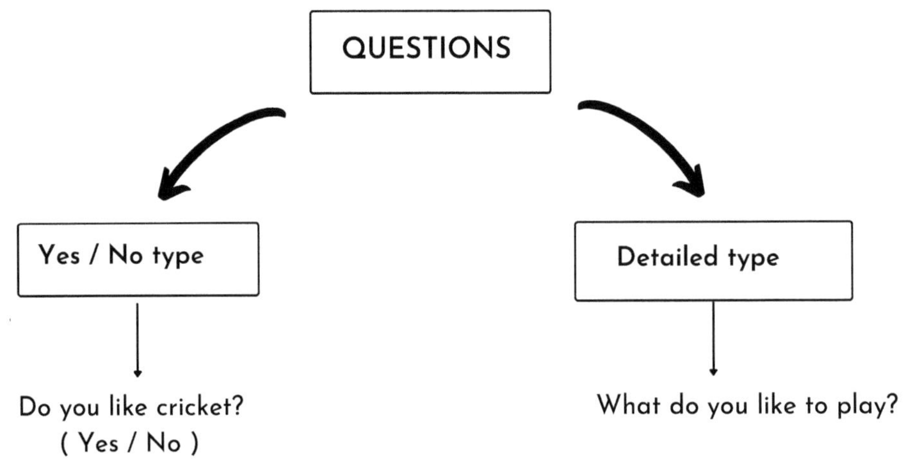

We use ***WH Family*** words to form only Detailed type questions.
The Yes/no type questions are formed from helping verbs.

1. **What**

It is used to

- ask questions
- as Relative pronoun (refers to "the things which")
- as Exclamation

eg:- ***What*** is your name?
What is Arithmetic?
My dad bought me ***what*** (the things which) I needed.
He gets ***what*** (the things which) he needs.
What! He has gone.

2. Who

It is used to

- ask questions (to know about someone)
- as Relative pronoun (refers to a person)

eg:- *Who* is your best friend?
Who comes with you?
The boy *who* is standing there is my brother.

3. Whom

It is used to

- used as an object (in questions)
- as a Relative pronoun.

eg:- *Whom* do you trust more, me or Suri?
The boy *whom* I gave the pencil was my best friend.

4. Why

It is used to

- ask Questions (to know the reason behind something)

eg:- *Why* are you doing this?
Why do you live in New York?
Why were you late?

5. Which

It is used to

- ask Questions (with reference to a non living things)
- as a Relative pronoun

eg:- *Which* is your favourite colour?
Which is your pen?
Which is the best laptop to buy?

6. When

It is used to

- ask Questions (about time)
- as a Relative pronoun

eg:- ***When*** did you go to America?
When do you have your classes?
When will you attend the classes?

7. Where

It is used to

- ask Questions (about place)
- as a Relative pronoun

eg:- ***Where*** did you live earlier?
Where are you going?
Where should we go now?

8. Whose

It is used to

- ask Questions (about belonging)
- as a Relative pronoun

eg:- ***Whose*** pen is this?
Whose keys are these?
Whose car is this?

9. How

It is used to

- ask Questions (about reason)
- as a Relative pronoun
- as How much (for uncountable nouns)
- as How many (for countable nouns)
- as How long (for duration)

eg:- ***How*** are you?
How much time does it take to go to Chennai via train?
How long will it take for my phone to be repaired?

PRACTICE EXERCISE

1. Form questions with the following sentences.

- It is his pen.
- Ramesh likes to play.
- Surbhi is knocking on the door.
- He doesn't know me.
- I don't know you.
- It takes 5 hours to go to Chennai.
- I'm fine.
- I lived in Cherrapunji earlier.
- He is doing his MBBS at a great reputed college.
- I agree with you.
- She gets to know everything.
- Virat Kohli won the title of fastest 100 this year.
- Henry is the most disturbing boy in the class.
- The city of Jaipur is the pink city of India.
- I make sculptures because I love to make them.
- My favourite colour is green.

Lesson #23

Subject-Verb Agreement

Verbs must agree in number and person with their subjects.

There are a few rules regarding subject-verb agreement.

Rule 1:- If a subject is singular, its verb must be singular (except I and You)

eg:- Ramesh ***plays*** cricket.
He ***lives*** in Chennai.

Rule 2:- If a subject is plural, its verb must be plural.

eg:- They ***play*** cricket.
We ***are*** going to the ground.

Rule 3:- If two subjects are joined by 'and', the verb must be plural

eg:- Gagan and Naresh ***are*** best ***friends***.
Gold and silver ***are*** precious ***metals***.

Rule 4:- If two subjects are joined by 'and', but if they suggest one idea or refer to the same person or thing, then the verb must be singular.

eg:- The actor and producer ***has*** arrived. (refers to the same person)
Bread and butter ***is*** his only food. (refers to the same idea)

Rule 5:- If two or more singular subjects are joined by or, nor, either…or, neither…nor, not only or but also, then the verb must be singular.

eg:- ***Either*** Sachin ***or*** Wasim is reading.
Happiness ***or*** sorrow is the result of our actions.

Rule 6:- If two or more plural subjects are joined by or, nor, either...or, neither...nor, not only or but also, then the verb must be plural.

eg:- ***Neither*** the teachers ***nor the students are*** present.
Either my Sisters ***or my brothers are*** hosting the party.

Rule 7:- If the subjects joined by or, nor, either...or, neither...nor, not only or but also, then the verb must agree with the nearer subject.

eg:- ***Either*** they ***or I am*** responsible.
Either I ***or they are*** responsible.

Rule 8:- Two nouns qualified by each or every, though connected by and, require a singular verb.

eg:- ***Each*** of the ***hens was*** sick.
Every boy and every girl ***was*** inquired.

Rule 9:- Some nouns that are plural in form, but singular in meaning, require s singular verbs.

eg:- ***The news is*** true.
The subject of ***mathematics is*** difficult for Raj.

PRACTICE EXERCISE

1. Write the correct verb for the following sentences.

- He ______ near my house. (live)
- Rohan and Sohan _____ best friends. (be)
- My friends _______ me. (trust)
- She ____ not care about her presence. (do)
- Either my classmates or he _____ looking at the matter.
- He or Sohan ______ making noise. (be)
- Each student ______ requested to be present tomorrow. (be)
- Himesh and his friends _____ made the project. (has)
- Dr. Dinesh ______ the blood samples yesterday. (collect)
- The leader and his brothers _______ to the same tribe. (belong)
- A lot of houses ________ collapsed in the storm. (has)
- An enormous sum of money _______ stolen. (be)
- Everyone ________ time to relax. (need)
- My friends who are in the band _________ me to play a musical instrument. (want)
- Your trousers ________ to be cleaned. (need)

2. Fill in the blanks with correct form of verb.

- Time and tide _________ for none. (wait)
- The house with its contents _________ burned. (is)
- Gold and silver _________ precious metals. (is)
- He and I _________ in this apartment. (live)
- Either David or William _________ to blame.
- The news he gave yesterday _________ true. (is)
- Optics _________ a branch of physics. (is)
- The quality of the mangoes _________ not good. (is)
- Each of the students in the hall _________ good marks. (score)
- Fire and water _________ not agree. (do)
- Everyone of my friends _________ to ride a bike. (love)
- The juggler and joker _________ too unwell to perform.
- Trilok says "No news _________ good news."(is)

Lesson #24

Tenses

Read the following sentences.

I *wake* up early in the morning.
I *woke* up early in the morning.
I *will wake* up early in the morning.

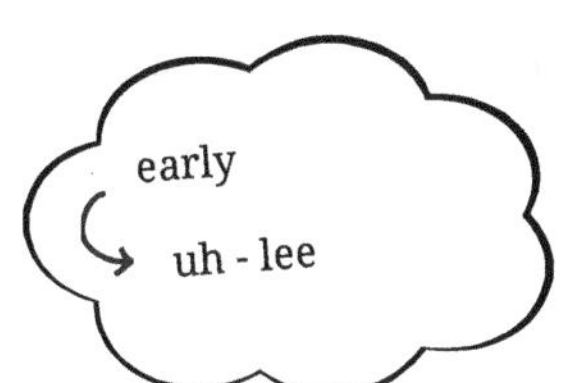

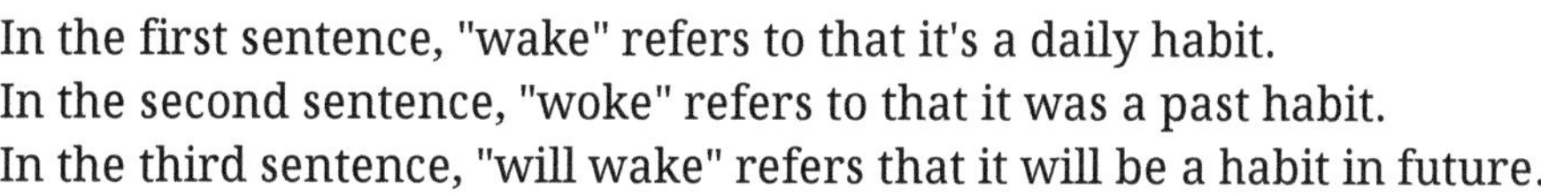
In the first sentence, "wake" refers to that it's a daily habit.
In the second sentence, "woke" refers to that it was a past habit.
In the third sentence, "will wake" refers that it will be a habit in future.

A tense is a grammar concept that describes when an action has been completed and how much of that action has been completed.

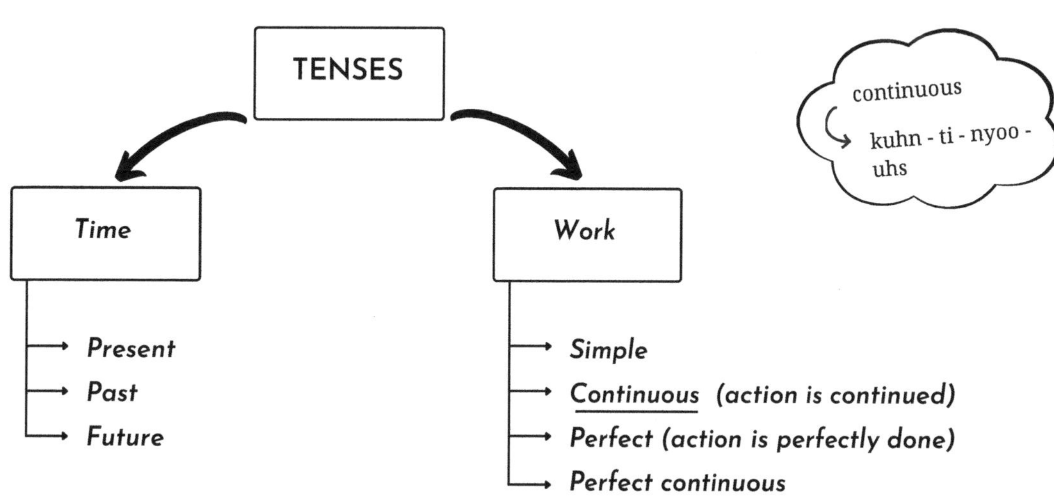

Let's see how tenses are formed by combining both time and work.

Present Tense	***Past Tense***	***Future Tense***
• Present Indefinite • Present Continuous • Present Perfect • Present Perfect Continuous	• Past Indefinite • Past Continuous • Past Perfect • Past Perfect Continuous	• Future Indefinite • Future Continuous • Future Perfect • Future Perfect Continuous

So, we have already covered the concept of Verbs in **Lesson#12.**

We have read there about helping verbs and main verbs and seen how can a perfect sentence be formed.

HOW TO RECOGNIZE WHEN THE WORK IS DONE?

We have seen that verbs can be classified based on time,i.e.,

1. ***Present tense***
2. ***Past tense***
3. ***Future tense***

So we must know how to form sentences and categorize them based on time.

*A sentence could be categorized based on time by using **"Helping verbs."***

We have already gone through the different kinds of helping verbs in the lesson.
Now, we will see where we should use them?

	Infinitive	*Continuous*	*Perfect*	*Perf. Continuous*
Present Tense	Do Does	Is Am Are	Has Have	Has been Have been
Past Tense	Did	Was Were	Had	Had been
Future Tense	Will Shall	Will be Shall be	Will have Shall have	Will have - been Shall have - been

HOW TO RECOGNIZE HOW MUCH THE WORK IS COMPLETED?

We have seen that work can be classified as infinitive, continuous, perfect and perfect continuous. But the question arrives, that how much the work is completed?
The completion of work can be determined by the **form of the main verbs**. We have already gone through the different forms of verbs in the Lesson.

The different forms of verbs indicate the different cases of work done.

First form	Infinitive (present + past)
Second form	Infinitive (past)
Third form	Perfect
Fourth form	Continuous

Let's know more about the tenses in brief.

PRESENT TENSE

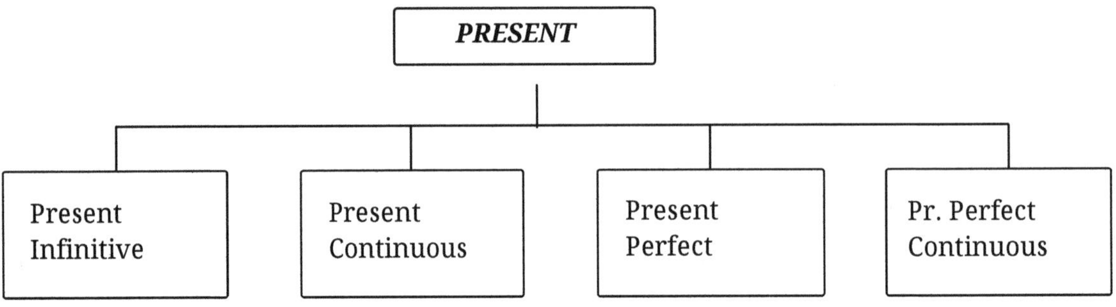

1. **Simple Present (Infinitive)**

   It is used to indicate

   - Habits
   - Natural truths
   - State or fact

natural
na - chuh - ruhl

Helping verb :- Do, Does
Main verb :- V1 (first form)

eg:- He reads a book.
They read a book.

In the first sentence, the verb "read" has a suffix "-s" with it.

NOTE :- 1. The helping verb of the simple present tense is mostly used with negative statements and questions.

2. If we use the first form of the verb with third-person singular pronouns (he, she, it) or with a name then we add '-s' or '-es' with the verb.

Formation of simple present sentences

- ***Statement :- Subject + V1(s/es) + object***

  eg :- He plays with ball.

- ***Negative statement :- Subject + do/does + not + V1 + object***

  eg :- He does not plays with ball.

- ***Interrogative statement :- <WH family> + Do/Does + Subject + V1 + object***

  eg :- Does he play with ball?

- ***Negative Interrogative statement :- <Wh family> + do/does + Subject + not + V1 + object***

  eg :- Why Does he not play with ball?

2. **Present Continuous**

   It is used to indicate

   - An action going at the time of speaking.

Helping verb:- Is (singular)
Am (I)
Are (plural + you)

Main verb :- V4 (fourth form)

eg:- I am writing a letter to my uncle.
You are going to school.
He is watching T.V.

Formation of Present Continuous sentences

- ***Statement :- Subject + is/am/are + V4 + object***

  eg :- She is baking a cake.

- ***Negative statement :- Subject + is/am/are + not + V4 + object***

  eg :- She is not baking a cake.

- ***Interrogative statement :- <Wh>+ Is/Am/Are + Subject + V4 + object***

  eg :- Is she baking a cake?

- ***Negative Interrogative statement :- Wh family + is/am/are Subject + not + V4 + object***

  eg :- Why is she not baking a cake?

NOTE:-

Some verbs usually do not have the fourth form (-ing form). These verbs are STATIVE VERBS :-

see, hear, taste, smell, appear, seem, want, wish, feel, love, hate, imagine, mind, understand, own, possess

3. **Present Perfect**

It is used to indicate

- An action completed in the immediate past (just before speaking).
- Past events when we think more of their effectiveness remain in the present.

Helping verb :- Has (singular)
Have (plural + I + you)

Main verb :- V3 (third form)

eg:- He has completed the work.
You have visited them...

Formation of present perfect sentences

- ***Statement :- Subject + has/have + V3 + object***

  eg :- We have finished the lunch.

- ***Negative statement :- Subject + has/have + not + V3 + object***

  eg :- We have not finished the lunch.

- ***Interrogative statement :- <WH> + Has/have + Subject + V3 + object***

  eg :- Have we finished the lunch?

- ***Negative Interrogative statement :- <WH> + Has/have + Subject + not + V3 + object***

  eg :- Why have we not finished the lunch?

4. Present Perfect Continuous

It is used to indicate

- An action that began at some time in the past and is continuing in the present.

Helping verb :- Has been (singular)
Have been (plural + I + you)

Main verb :- V4 (fourth form)

eg:- He has been reading since 2 p.m.
I have been watching T.V. for two hours.
You have been playing cricket for three hours.

Formation of Present Perfect Continuous sentences

- ***Statement :- Subject + has/have + been + V4 + object***
  eg :- They have been talking since 4p.m.

- ***Negative statement :- Subject + has/have + not + been+ V4 + object***
  eg :- They have not been talking since 4 p.m.

- ***Interrogative statement :- <WH> +Has/have + Subject + been + V4 + object***
  eg :- Have they been talking since 4p.m.?

- ***Negative Interrogative statement :- <WH> + has/have + Subject + not + been + V3 + object***
  eg :- Why have they not been talking since 4 p.m.?

NOTE:- "Since" and "For" are used in perfect continuous tenses to indicate the time at which the action was started or ended.

SINCE is used to indicate a point of time when the action was started or was continuous.
eg:- He has been sleeping since 5 a.m.
We have been watching T.V. since 4 p.m.

FOR is used to indicate a duration of time when the action was started or was continuous.
eg:- He has been sleeping for 6 hours.
We have been watching T.V. for 3 hours.

PAST TENSE

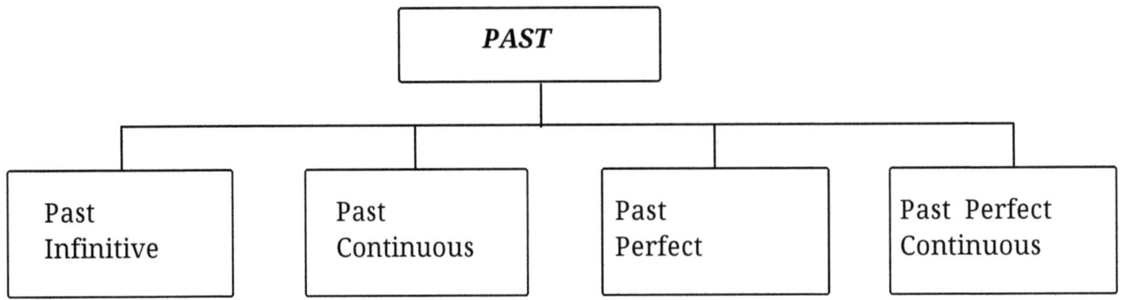

1. **Past Simple (Infinitive)**

   It is used to indicate

   - An action completed in past.
   - Past habits

   Helping verb :- Did

   Main verb :- V1 (if did is used)
   V2 (if did is not used)

   eg:- She left the school last month.
   He talked very gently. (past habit)
   I did not go to the office yesterday.

Formation of Past simple sentences

- ***Statement :- Subject + V2 + object***

  eg :- I went to Kashmir last week.

- ***Negative statement :- Subject + did+ not + V1 + object***

  eg :- I did not go to Kashmir last week.

- ***Interrogative statement :- <WH> + Did+ Subject + V1 + object***

  eg :- Did I go to Kashmir last week?

- ***Negative Interrogative statement :- <WH> + did+ Subject + V1 + object***

  eg :- Where did I go last week?

2. Past Continuous

It is used to indicate

- some action that was in progress at a certain moment in the past and either finished in the past or continued until the present moment.

Helping verb :- Was
Were

Main verb :- V4

eg:- We were working on our office project.
I was playing in the park.
It was making very noise when you left for the office.

Formation of Past Continuous sentences

- ***Statement :- Subject + was/were + V4 + object***
  eg :- He was cooking food.

- ***Negative statement :- Subject + was/were + not + V4 + object***
  eg :- He was not cooking food.

- ***Interrogative statement :- <WH> + was/were + Subject + V4 + object***
  eg :- What was he cooking ?

- ***Negative Interrogative statement :- <WH> + was/were + Subject + not + V4 + object***
  eg :- Why was he not cooking food?

3. **Past Perfect**

It is used to indicate

- something occurred before another action in the past
- something happened before a specific time in the past.

Helping verb :- Had

Main verb :- V3

eg:- He had left his keys in the house when he left.
The film had ended when I switched on the television.
Had you gone to London the last week when I was sick?

Formation of Past Perfect sentences

- ***Statement :- Subject*** + ***had*** + ***V3*** + ***object***
  eg :- He had gone home as I came.

- ***Negative statement :- Subject*** + ***had*** + ***not*** + ***V3*** + ***object***
  eg :- He had not gone home as I came.

- ***Interrogative statement :-*** <***WH***> + ***had*** + ***Subject*** + ***V3*** + ***object***
  eg :- Why had he gone to home as I came?

- ***Negative Interrogative statement :-*** <***WH***> + ***had*** + ***Subject*** + ***not*** + ***V3*** + ***object***
  eg :- Why had he not gone home as I came?

4. **Past Perfect Continuous**

It is used to indicate

- An action that began and was still in progress in the past before another past action started.

Helping verb :- Had been

Main verb :- V3

eg:- We had been waiting for a long time before the bus finally came
She had not been feeling well, so she went to lay down.
How long had you been staying in Europe after you got a job in America?

Formation of Past Perfect Continuous sentences

- ***Statement :- Subject* + *had* + *been* + *V4* + *object***

  eg :- He had been studying in India before he got a job in the UK.

- ***Negative statement :- Subject* + *had* + *not* + *been* + *V4* + *object***

  eg :- He had not been studying in India before he got a job in the UK.

- ***Interrogative statement :-*** *<WH>* + ***had* + *Subject* + *been* + *V4* + *object***

  eg :- Had he been studying in India before he got a job in the UK.

- ***Negative Interrogative statement :-*** *<WH>* + ***had* + *Subject* + *not* + *been* + *V4* + *object***

  eg :-Where had he not been studying before he got a job in the UK.

FUTURE TENSE

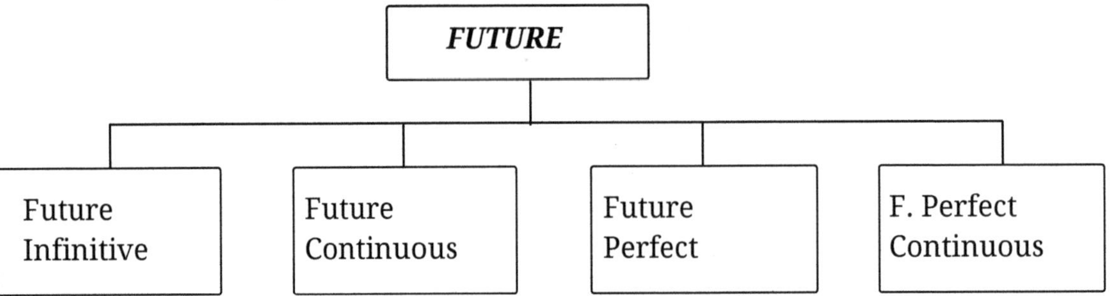

1. **Future Simple (Infinitive)**

   It is used to indicate
   - A future fact
   - A prediction
   - Promises

   Helping verb :- Will / Shall
   Main verb :- V1

   eg:- I will go to Russia the next month.
   They will come to my birthday party tomorrow.
   Shall I help you with your work?

Formation of Future Simple sentences

- ***Statement :- Subject + will/shall + V1 + object***

  eg :- It will rain tomorrow.

- ***Negative statement :- Subject + will/shall + not + V1 + object***

  eg :- It will not rain tomorrow.

- ***Interrogative statement :- <WH> + will/shall + Subject + V1 + object***

  eg :- Will it rain tomorrow?

- ***Negative Interrogative statement :- <WH> + will/shall + Subject + not + V1 + object***

  eg :-Why it will not rain tomorrow?

2. **Future Continuous**

It is used to indicate

- An unfinished action occurring in the future.
- This action can either begin in the future, or it can already be in progress in the present and continue into the future.

Helping verb :- Will be , Shall be

Main verb :- V4

eg:- I will be running the marathon tomorrow.
The plane will be landing in 10 minutes.
Will you be joining us after the show?

Formation of Future Continuous sentences

- ***Statement :- Subject*** + ***will /shall*** + ***be*** + ***V4*** + ***object***

  eg :- You will be coming with us tomorrow.

- ***Negative statement :- Subject*** + ***will /shall*** + ***not*** + ***be*** + ***V4*** + ***object***

  eg :- You will not be coming with us tomorrow.

- ***Interrogative statement :-*** <WH> + ***will /shall*** + ***Subject*** + ***be*** + ***V4*** + ***object***

  eg :- Why will he be coming with us tomorrow?

- ***Negative Interrogative statement :-*** <WH> + ***will/shall*** + ***Subject*** + ***not*** + ***be*** + ***V 4*** + ***object***

  eg :- Why will he not be coming with us tomorrow?

3. **Future Perfect**

It is used to indicate

- something will finish or be completed at a specific point of time in the future.

Helping verb :- Will have . Shall have

Main verb :- V3

eg:- This June, I will have lived in the UK for two years.
It's hard to believe that by next month we'll have been married for 10 years.
Who will have prepared the notes for the seminar?

Formation of Future Perfect sentences

- ***Statement :- Subject + will/shall + have + V3 + object***

  eg;- I will have done this work by evening.

- ***Negative statement :- Subject + will /shall + not + have + V3 + object***

  eg:- I will not have done this work by evening.

- ***Interrogative statement :- <WH> + will /shall + Subject + have + V3 + object***

  eg:- How I will have done this work by evening?

- ***Negative Interrogative statement :- <WH> + will/shall + Subject + not +have + V3 + object***

  eg:- How will I not have done this work by evening?

4. **Future Perfect Continuous**

It is used to indicate

- how long something has been happening once a future moment in time is reached.

Helping verb :- Will have been / Shall have been

Main verb :- V4

eg:- I will have been working there for more than half my life when I will turn 30.

Formation of Future Perfect Continuous sentences

- ***Statement :- Subject** + **will/shall** + **have been** + **V4** + **object***

  eg :- He will have been studying in India before he got a job in the UK.

- ***Negative statement :- Subject** + **will/shall** + **not** + **have been** + **V4** + **object***

  eg :- He will not have been studying in India before he got a job in the UK.

- ***Interrogative statement :- <WH>** + **will/shall** + **Subject** + **have been** + **V4** + **object***

  eg :- Where will he have been studying before he got a job in the UK?

- ***Negative Interrogative statement :- <WH>** + **will/shall** + **Subject** + **not** + **have been** + **V3** + **object***

  eg :- Where will he not have been studying before he got a job in the UK?

TENSES CHART

TENSES	*Helping Verb*	*Main Verb*	*Examples*
Present Simple	Do Does	V1 V1 + s, es (with 3rd person singular)	He plays with a ball. Does he play with a ball? You play with a ball.
Present Continuous	Is Am Are	V4 (V1 + ing)	He is playing with a ball. Is he playing with a ball? You are playing with a ball.
Present Perfect	Has Have	V3	He has played with a ball. Has he played with a ball? You have played with a ball.
Present Per. Continuous	Has been Have been	V4 (V1 + ing)	He has been playing with a ball for 2 hours. Has he been playing with a ball for 2 hours?
Past Simple	Did	V1 (if did is used) V2	He played with a ball. Did he play with a ball? You played with a ball.
Past Continuous	Was Were	V4 (V1 + ing)	He was playing with a ball. Was he playing with a ball? You were playing with a ball.
Past Perfect	Had	V3	He had played with a ball. Had he played with a ball? You had played with a ball.

TENSES	*Helping Verb*	*Main Verb*	*Examples*
Past Per. Continuous	Had been	V4 (V1 + ing)	He had been playing with a ball for 2 hours. Had he been playing with a ball for 2 hours?
Future Simple	Will Shall	V1	He will play with a ball. Will he play with a ball? You will play with a ball.
Future Continuous	Will be Shall be	V4 (V1 + ing)	He will be playing with a ball. Will he be playing with a ball? You will be playing with a ball.
Future Perfect	Will have Shall have	V3	He will have played with a ball. Will he have played with a ball? You will have played with a ball.
Future Per. Continuous	Will have been Shall have been	V4 (V1 + ing)	He will have been playing with a ball for 2 hours. Will he have been playing with a ball for 2 hours?

PRACTICE EXERCISES

1. Fill in the blanks with the correct form of verbs.

- My sister ________ (read) a book.
- Frank _________ (like) dogs.
- My parents _________ (do) the shopping.
- We sometimes _________ (meet) in front of the cinema.
- Uncle George _________ (go) to the park.
- Our friends _________ (play) football in the park.
- Yesterday evening I _________ (watch) TV.
- I only _________ (brush) my teeth four times last week.
- The concert last night _________ (start) at 7.30 and _________ (end) at 10 o'clock.
- The accident _________ (happen) last Sunday afternoon.
- She _________ (sleep) now.
- Sarvesh and Ravi __________ (sing) in the auditorium yesterday.
- We ____________ (watch) the live cricket match yesterday.
- _____ you __________ (eat) the lunch in the canteen now?
- He ___ played football.
- They ________ (listen) songs since 3p.m.

2. Form questions for the following sentences.

- I am playing cricket.
- He is ill.
- Ram goes to the market.
- He loves tea.
- I will learn to swim.
- You have attended the meeting.
- She will be hosting the event next week.
- I had come to you.
- She has been painting since morning.
- Sam was swimming with me yesterday morning.
- The bowl is green.

3. Write the type of tense and then convert it into another tense accordingly,

- My father reads the newspaper. (Change into present continuous)
- Sarvesh is dreaming in his sleep. (Change into present simple)
- Do you love painting? (Change into past simple)
- Mr Sharma and his family have lived here for 24 years. (Change into past perfect)
- I will come with you. (Change into future perfect)
- Ask him if he wants a cup of tea. (Change into past simple)
- She is going to Bangalore next week. (Change into future simple)
- I will be writing my exam this time tomorrow. (Change into past continuous tense)
- She hadn't thought about that. (Change into simple past)

- He will wait for us. (Change into present continuous tense)
- He will not pass the test. (Change into future perfect tense)
- The boy got up late and missed the bus. (Change into future simple)
- The baby cried for hours. (Change into present perfect continuous)
- Priya shall finish her stitching by then. (Change into past perfect continuous)
- Have I been to Sid's house yesterday? (Change into Past simple)

4. Fill in the blanks with correct form of verbs.

- When I arrive home, my dog __________ for me. (wait)
- I like to __________ (draw)
- I'm sure you __________ the exam. (pass)
- I __________ here till Saturday. (stay)
- The film __________ at noon (start)
- When I visited her, she __________ her meal. (eat)
- He __________ fast when the accident happened. (drive)
- I __________a strange noise (hear)
- We __________ our breakfast an hour ago. (finish)
- This __________ every day. (happen)
- When I was in Sri Lanka, I __________ Negombo, Beruwala and Nilaveli. (visit)
- I __________ (sleep) since 7 a.m. and you didn't even __________ (try) to wake me up.
- When Mr Richard came to school in 2005, Mr Vishnu __________ there for five years. (teach)
- It __________ darker. (get)
- Jane already __________ (type) three pages when her computer ____________. (crash)
- I ____________ to Canada so far. (be)
- By 10 o'clock, we ____________ our work. (finish)
- I ____________ start my new project tomorrow. (start)

Lesson #25

Modals

Verbs were introduced in Lesson #12. We have already learned that verbs can be divided into helping and main verbs. Further, helping verbs are classified into two types: auxiliaries and modals.

Modals are words that are used as helping verbs in a sentence. They express meanings such as permission, possibility, ability, certainty. Common modals include, will, shall, may, and can.

Let's check out the different modals and their usage. The modals would be classified according to their meanings and what they express.

1. **Permission**

   The modal verbs used to ask permission are:-
   - Can (Informal)
   - May (Formal)
   - Could (Formal)

   eg:- *May* I come in sir? (Formal)
   Can I use our phone, Raman? (Informal)
   Could you please give me a glass of water? (Formal)

   The modal verbs used to give permission are:-
   - Can (Informal)
   - May (Formal)

   eg:- Yes, you *may* come in. (Formal)
   Yes, Raman, you *can* use my phone. (Informal)

2. Ability

The modal verbs used to show or judge someone's or something's ability are:-

- Can (Present and future)
- Could (Past)

eg:- I ***can*** lift that box. (present ability)
I ***could*** lift that box when I was a kid. (past ability)
I ***can*** do this work tomorrow. (future ability)

3. Possibility

The modal verbs used to show or guess possibility about something are:-

- May (high possibility)
- Might (low possibility)
- Could (low possibility)

eg:- It ***may*** rain today. (high possibility)
It ***might*** rain today. (low possibility)

The modal verbs used to show or guess impossibility about something are:-

- Cannot / Can't

eg:- It ***cannot*** rain today.

4. Certainty

The modal verbs used to show certainty are:-

- Must
- Should

eg:- He ***must*** be there.
Sheetal ***should*** be present today.

5. Request

The modal verbs used to request someone for something are:-

- Can
- Will

} It's less polite

- Could
- Would

} It's more polite

eg:- ***Can*** you help me? (less polite)
Could you help me? (more polite)

6. Future

The modal verbs used to speak about the future are:-

- Will
- Shall

eg:- He ***will*** go to the stadium.
They ***shall*** go to the stadium.

7. Offer

The modal verbs used to offer something to someone are:-

- Shall
- Can

eg:- ***Shall*** I help you?

8. Suggestion / Obligation

The modal verbs used for the suggestion or to speak about duties are:-

- Must (order or compulsion)
- Should (advice)

eg:- School uniforms ***must*** be worn in class.
You ***should*** do your work.

PRACTICE EXERCISES

1. **Fill in the blanks with correct modal verbs.**

- _________ (need, can, will) you lend me your cycle?
- He _________ (can, could, should) lift the box.
- I _________ (should, could, would) run faster when I was young.
- She _________ (may, will, dare) achieve her goals.
- You _________ (must, should, would) exercise more often.
- _________ (may, can, could) I come in, sir?
- It _________ (should, might, can) rain today.
- The children _________ (should, must, need to) obey their parents.
- I _________ (cannot, could not, will) write what you spoke.
- I _________ (would, could, should) love to teach these children.
- _________ (will, could, can) I have a cup of tea.
- Somebody _________ (must, dare, should) have told him.
- _________ (could, should, may) you open the window, please?
- You _________ (can, need not, will not) come to my office. Just ring me up.
- Mohan went to Agra last week. He _________ (can, may, might) come today.
- My teacher_________ (can/must) speak four languages.
- _________ (May/should) I use your mobile to call my mother?
- You _________ (must/could) not speak loudly in the hospital.
- I _________ (could/must) use a little help in packing all these clothes.
- Madam _________ (could/may) you repeat what you said?
- I _________ (can/might) not be able to make it tonight.
- I _________ (will/must) succeed in the attempt.
- Where _________ (can/may) he have gone?

Lesson #26

Active Passive Voice

The language we use plays a key role in expressing our ideas.
The ideas can be conveyed in different ways. Here, the concept of Voice plays a very important role in conveying our ideas differently.

Read the following examples and compare.

Hari is playing the flute.
The flute is being played by Ravi.

Both sentences convey the same meaning but are expressed differently.
In the first sentence, the subject is more focused than the verb, therefore it is in the active voice.
In the second sentence, the verb is more focused than the subject, therefore it is in the passive voice.

Voice, in grammar, is a form of a verb that describes whether the subject acts upon its verb (active voice) or the verb acts upon the subject (passive verb).

Types of Voice

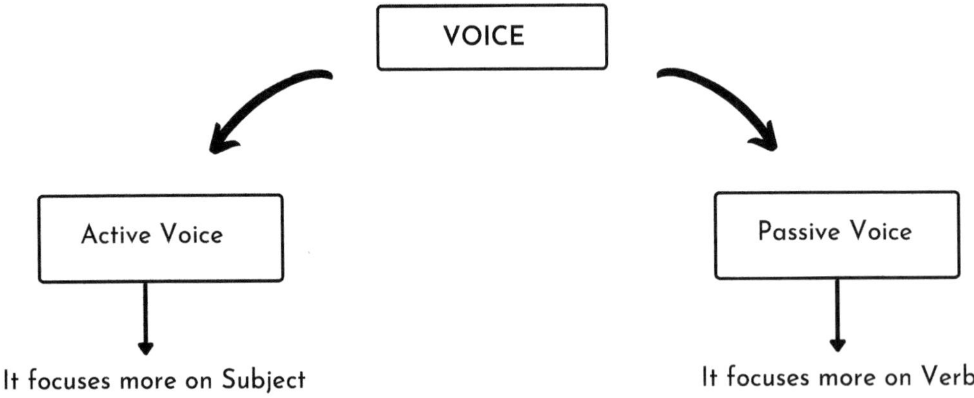

The interesting thing is that we have already covered the Active voice in previous chapters. It is like any other normal sentence.

Now, we have to learn more about Passive voice.

FORMATION OF PASSIVE VOICE

The very simple rule to form passive voice is to just interchange the structure of a simple sentence.

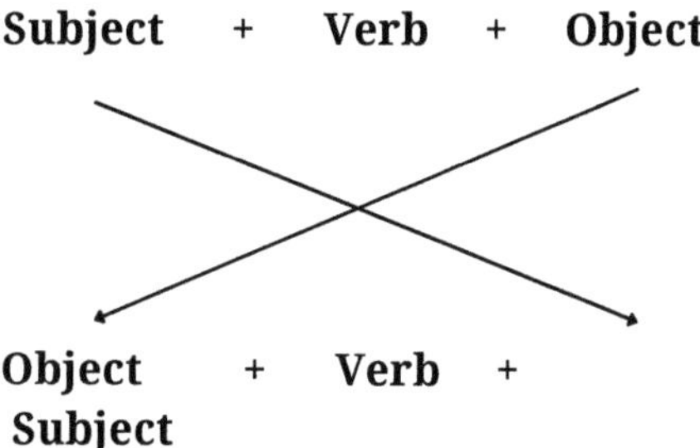

There will be a simple change in the form of the helping verb, but the main verb is always the third form of the verb in the passive voice.

The helping verb of a passive form is decided by the number and person of the object used in the active form.

Here is the table which shows the change in form of verbs.

Active Voice	Passive Voice	Examples
Simple Present	Present continuous	takes - is taken
Present continuous	No change in H.V. but ' being is added after the helping verb.	is taking - is being taken
Present perfect	Present perfect continuous	has taken - has been taken
Present perfect continuous	Not used in passive	
Simple Past	Past continuous	took - was taken

Active Voice	Passive Voice	Examples
Past continuous	No change in H.V. but ' being is added after the helping verb.	was taking - was being taken
Past perfect	Past perfect continuous	had taken - had been taken
Past perfect continuous	Not used in passive	

Some Examples (The words in brackets inform about the helping verb, not the main verb)

Active :- Soham plays football. (Simple present)
Passive :- Football is played by Soham. (Present continuous)

Active :- Soham is playing football. (Present continuous)
Passive :- Football is being played by Soham.

Active :- Soham has played football. (Present perfect)
Passive :- Football has been played by Soham. (Present perfect cont.)

Active :- Soham played football. (Simple present)
Passive :- Football was played by Soham. (Past cont.)

Active :- Soham was playing football. (Past cont)
Passive :- Football was being played by Soham.

Active :- Soham had played football. (Past perfect)
Passive :- Football had been played by Soham. (Past perfect cont.)

PRACTICE EXERCISES

1. **Change the active sentences below into passive sentences.**

- She writes a letter.
- They go to school every day.
- Why are you crying?
- Did the mechanic fix your car?
- You should do your homework.
- They are painting their house.
- We have drunk milk tea.
- Will you watch TV tonight?
- I will not work today.
- He has been teaching English for ten years.
- When are you going to buy a car?
- Who taught you the active and passive sentences?
- She had cleaned the kitchen.
- We will have eaten dinner by the time you get there.
- People speak English in the USA.

2. **Change the passive sentences below into active sentences.**

- A novel is read.
- The words are explained by the teacher today.
- We were sent a letter the day before yesterday.
- This car will not be stolen. It's too old.
- This street has already been closed because of snow.
- A new restaurant will be opened next week.
- He was invited to the party yesterday.
- The blue box cannot be seen.
- I was given the book by my friend last Sunday.
- The dishes have not been washed by my little brother.
- I will not be asked by Robert.
- This house was built in 1943 by my grandfather.
- The traffic might have delayed Jimmy.
- You will be told later by John
- My wallet must have been taken

3. Fill in the blanks.

1. Fiat _______________ (started) by a group of Italian businessmen in 1899. In 1903, Fiat, 1 _______________ (produced) 132 cars. Some of these cars 2 c (exported) by the company to the United States and Britain. In 1920, Fiat 3 _______________ (started) making cars at a new factory at Lingotto, near Turin. There was a track on the roof where the cars 4 _________________ (tested) by technicians. In 1936, Fiat launched the Fiat 500. This car 5 _________________ (called) the Topolino – the Italian name for Mickey Mouse. The company grew, and in 1963 Fiat 6 ___________________ (exported) more than 300,000 vehicles. Today, Fiat is based in Turin, and its cars 7 _______________ (sold) all over the world.

2. Two men _____________________ (see) breaking into a house in my street last night. The police __________________ (call) and they arrived very quickly. One man __________________ (catch) immediately. The other escaped, but he ___________________ (find) soon. Both men __________________ (take) to the police station where they ______________________ (question) separately by a police officer. The two men _____________________ (charge) with burglary.

4. Convert the following into passive sentences.

1. Someone broke into a local jewellery shop yesterday. The owner had just locked up the shop when a robber with a gun threatened him. The robber told him to unlock the shop and give him all the diamonds in the safe. Then the robber tied him up. The police have organized a search for the robber. They hope they will find him in a few days. Doctors are treating the owner of the shop for shock.

   ____

2. My uncle painted this picture. Someone has offered him a lot of money for it. He will deliver the painting tomorrow. When they give him the money, he will tell them the truth. He painted it one night while he was sleepwalking! ____________________

Lesson #27

Direct Indirect Speech

Speech is an important aspect of communication.
We may present the words of a speaker in two ways:

1. We may present his actual words. This is called ***Direct Speech***
2. We may not present his actual words but we may present them with some modifications. This is called ***Indirect speech.***

eg:- Divya said, "I am ill." (Direct speech)
Divya said that she was ill. (Indirect speech)

The sentences in Direct speech have two parts:

1. **Reported verb**
2. **Reported speech**

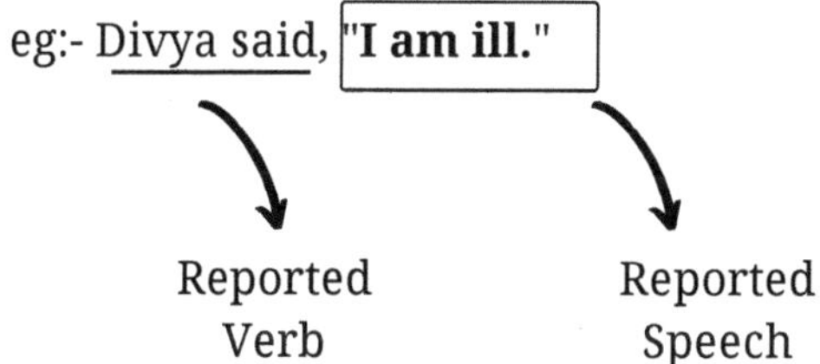

RULES FOR CHANGING DIRECT SPEECH INTO INDIRECT

STATEMENTS

- Reporting verb 'said to' is changed in told, replied, asked, advised, etc.
- After the reporting verb, the conjunction, 'that' or 'if/whether' is used to join both parts.
- The pronouns used in the reported speech change accordingly.
  1st person changes according to the subject
  2nd person changes according to the object
  3rd person is not changed.

- When the reporting verb is in the past tense, the tense of reported speech is changed accordingly.

Direct speech	Indirect speech
Simple present	Simple past
Present continuous	Past continuous
Present perfect	Past perfect
Present perfect continuous	Past perfect continuous
Simple past	Past perfect
Past continuous	Past perfect continuous

Some Examples

Direct :- Dinesh said,"I am happy."
Indirect :- Dinesh said that he was happy.

CHANGES:-

1. Use of 'that'.
2. 'I' is changed into 'he'. (1st person changes according to the subject)
3. The helping verb 'am' is changed into 'was'.

Direct :- He said, "I am going to the USA."
Indirect :- He said that he was going to the USA.

Direct :- Hemant said, "She looks pretty."
Indirect :- Hemant said that she looked pretty.

Direct :- Viraj said, "We have won the match."
Indirect :- Viraj said that they had won the match.

Direct :- She said, "I have never seen this picture."
Indirect :- She said that she had never seen this picture.

Some specific words are changed

Now	- Then	Today	- That day
Her	- There	Yesterday	- The previous day
Ago	- Before	Tomorrow	- The next day
Thus	- So	Last night	- The night before

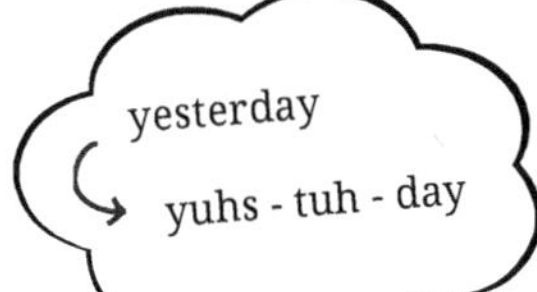

QUESTIONS

- Reporting verb is changed to 'asked'.
- 2. Reporting verb and the reporting speech are joined by 'if' or 'whether' if the question doesn't start with 'Wh family'.

Some examples

Direct :- Alex said, "Is he going to Bengaluru?"
Indirect :- Alex asked if he was going to Bengaluru.

Direct :- She said to me, "What is your name?"
Indirect :- She asked me what was my name.

Direct :- I said to Raj, "Will he go to the party?"
Indirect :- I asked Raj whether he would go to the party..

IMPERATIVES (COMMANDS AND REQUESTS)

- Reporting verb is changed to 'ordered', 'commanded', 'suggested that', 'advised'.
- The structure for this type of indirect speech would be:

  Speaker + **Reporting verb** + **Object** + **to** + **....**

Some examples

Direct :- Selena said to him, "Shut the door."
Indirect :- Selena ordered him to shut the door.

Direct :- She said to me, "You should visit a doctor."
Indirect :- She suggested that I should visit a doctor.

EXCLAMATIONS AND WISHES

- Reporting verb is changed to 'exclaimed with joy / sorrow / regret / surprise'. And 'that' is used to join both parts.

Some examples

Direct :- Manas said, "Hurrah! We won the match."
Indirect :- Manas exclaimed with joy that they had won the match.

Direct :- She said, "Alas! He is dead"
Indirect :- She exclaimed with sorrow that he was dead.

PRACTICE EXERCISES

1. **Change the following sentences into indirect speech.**

- "I'll have a cup of tea," my father said, "because I'm not hungry."
- Father said to me, "May you pass the examination"
- He remarked, "Two and two make four."
- The men said, "We are going to fly kites."
- He said, "I have been studying in this college for two years."
- She said to me, "Have you finished your work?"
- Jonah said, "I don't like your hat."
- They asked my brother, "What do you do?"
- He told me, "Be quiet!"
- Mother said, "I have a headache."
- He asked her, "Do you know the right way?"
- She asked him, "Where have you lost your camera?"
- She asked him, "Where have you lost your camera?"
- He said to me, "Don't play music here."
- She said to me, "Shut the door."
- He write and said, "I am unable to come just now because I am ill, but I will certainly start my work as soon as I am well enough to do so."
- "I know her address",said Gopi.

2. **Change the following sentences into direct speech.**

- The teacher told the student that he might buy that book if he liked it.
- Mala told her friends that she would wait for them if they were late.
- The teacher ordered Rakesh to go out and not to come again to the class.
- The guide asked the tourist if he wanted to see the Taj.
- Ravi asked his sister why she was not doing her work properly.
- He requested me to wait there till he returned.
- The teacher ordered us to stop that noise in the class.
- Sushila asked the visitor what he ate for breakfast.
- Father advised me not to be rude to anyone.
- The shopkeeper asked what he wanted.
- The manager asked the clerk to post those letters that day.
- Gopal proposed that they should have a cup of tea.
- The captain advised the players to play the game fairly.
- Satish requested Ram to lend him his book for a day.
- Kanta told her father that she had visited the zoo the previous day.
- I asked Mary if she could lend me a pencil.
- He replied that he had promised to reward his soldiers and that he had kept his word.

3. **Change the following dialogues into indirect speech.**

1. Father: Why ask so many questions, Latha?
   Latha: I believe that if you don't know the answer, keep asking till you do!

2. "It doesn't matter," Joan said.
   "It does to me," said Brandon

3. Hari:- Did you see my new umbrella?
   Vikas:- Yes, It is beautiful. Where did you buy it from?
   Hari:- My father bought it for me from the supermarket.

4. Child- Good Morning Sir, how are you?
   Teacher- I am completely fine. What about you?
   Student- I was wondering which course to learn in my vacation.
   Teacher- It can be confusing with so many options online. You should make a list and narrow it down as per your interest.
   Student- I have tried that but still I am left with three options- Artificial Intelligence, Machine learning or Data science.
   Teacher- Well! All of them are very interesting courses, but as far as I remember you have always been interested in Artificial Intelligence.
   Student- Yes! I do because I feel it is our future.
   Teacher- Well then its no harm in pursuing it and later if you find it less interesting you can always switch.
   Student- Yes it sounds like a great idea. Thanks!

3. **Change the following dialogues into direct speech.**

1. I told Harry that Sean was looking for him. Harry replied he doesn't want to talk to him as he was angry with him. I asked whether they fought or something like that. Harry said that Sean was dishonest with him and he had also stolen his gold chain.

2. The teacher instructed Samir to draw a biological plant cell on the board and asked him if he knew the diagram. Samir respectfully answered that he knew the diagram but he hesitated if it was correct. The teacher asked to continue. Samir finally drew the cell and asked his teacher whether it was correct. His teacher replied that he has drawn the correct diagram.

PART - 3
VOCABULARY

Lesson #28

Pronunciation

It's important to pronounce every word and sentence properly.
Most of us aren't aware of the correct pronunciation of some words which sometimes alter the meaning of the word you speak.
So, here we will go through the correct pronunciations of every letter briefly.

Pronunciation of Vowels

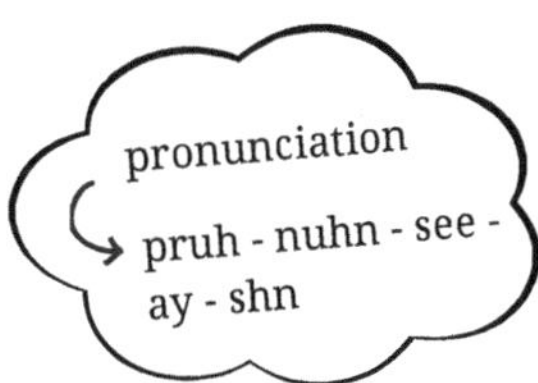

We have already gone through vowels in Lesson#1.
The vowels are A, E, I, O, U.

PRONUNCIATION OF "A"

	Sound	Examples
	A, AI, AY (short sound)	Rain, Shape, Fame, Blame
	A (long sound)	Ash, Trash, Mat, Hat
	A {uh} (long sound)	Alert, Agree
	Aeh	Rare, Dare, Care
	Aa	Are, After, Car
	Aw	Tall, Crawl, Shawl

PRONUNCIATION OF "E"

	Sound	Examples
	E (short sound)	Hen, Men, Set
	E, Ee (long sound)	Eagle, Ear, East
	E {Eh}	Elephant, Egg
	Ew	Few, Dew

PRONUNCIATION OF "I"

	Sound	Examples
	I (short sound)	Bill, Mill, Hill
	I (long sound)	Receive
	I {ai}	Grinder, Bike
	I (uh)	Birth, Shirt
	Ie (ee)	Niece, Piece
	Io (aay)	Lion, Riot

PRONUNCIATION OF "O"

	Sound	Examples
	O (short sound)	More, Old, Bold
	Oo (short sound)	Cook, Look, Took
	Oo (Long sound)	Too, Shoot, Boot
	O (a)	Oppose, Son
	O (aw)	On, Hop, Shop, Job

PRONUNCIATION OF "U"

	Sound	Examples
	U (short sound)	Bull, Pull
	U (long sound)	Blue, Suit
	U (a)	Sun, Burn, Turn
	U (you)	Use, Salute, Cube
	U (yo)	Sure, Cure, Pure

NOTE :- Learning how to pronounce letters and words from a book can be quite difficult. We should be able to practice it in the best possible way. There is a great way to learn pronunciation.
It is possible to learn how to say every letter correctly.
Use Google whenever it is necessary.

SILENT LETTERS

The silent letter is a letter that does not correspond to a particular sound in a word in an alphabetic writing system.

Letters	***Rules***	***Examples***
A	When the word ends with -ally	Magically, Critically magically → mah - ji - kuh - lee
B	• When the word ends with -mb • When the word ends with -bt	Comb, Bomb Doubt, Debt bomb → bawm
C	After an 'S' and before an 'E' or an 'I'	Science, Descent science → saai - uhns
D	When -dg is used in a word	Bridge, Pledge pledge → pluhj
G	• When the word ends with -gn • When -gh is used after a vowel	Design, Foreign Fight, Night foreign → faw - ruhn
H	• When the word begins with 'Gh' • When the word begins with 'Rh' • Sometimes after a 'C' • Sometimes when a word starts with 'H'	Ghost, Ghetto ghost → gost Rhythm School, Chemistry Honest, Heir, Hour
I	*It is not silent normally. But there are some random words where it is silent.*	Business business → biz - nuhs

Letters	*Rules*	*Examples*
K	When the word begins with 'Kn'	Knee, Know knee → nee
L	*There is no definite rule here. But there are some random words which have a silent 'L'*	Calf, Walk, Talk, Chalk chalk → chawk
N	When the word ends with '-mn'	Autumn, Condemn autumn → aw - tum
P	When the word begins with 'Ps' , 'Pt' and 'Pn'	Psychology, Pneumonia pneumonia → new - moh - nia
S	*There is no definite rule here. But there are some random words which have a silent 'L'*	Island, Aisle, Isle island → aih - land
T	• Before '-ch' • If a word ends in '-sten' • Ifa word ends in '-stle'	Catch, Watch, Hatch Listen, Fasten Castle, Hustle castle → ka - sl
U	Often after a 'G' and before a vowel	Guest, Guard, Colleague colleague → kuh - leeg
W	When the word begins with 'Wr'	Wrong, Write

Lesson #29

Contractions

Contractions mean to shorten a word or phrase by omitting one or more sounds or letters from it.

We have already gone through Contractions in Lesson#5.

Important Contractions		
Is	's	It's , She's , He's (It is , She is ....)
Am	'm	I'm (I am)
Are	're	We're , They're (We are , They are)
Have	've	We've , They've (We have ....)
Has	's	It's , She's , He's (It has , She has ....)
Had	'd	I'd , He'd , We'd (I had, He had .....)
Would	'd	They'd , She'd , (They would....)
Will	'll	He'll , I'll , We'll (He will , I will)

Here are some more contractions with their examples.

1. Let us = Let's

eg:- Let's go for a walk.
Let's play.
Let's have a party tonight.
Let's do it.

2. That is = That's

eg:- That's it. (That is it)
That's good. (That is good)
That's my brother. (That is my brother)

3. What is = What's

eg:- What's the matter?
What's going here?
What's happening?

4. The nots:

hasn't = has not
isn't = is not
don't = do not
doesn't = does not
won't = will not
haven't = have not
can't = can not
wouldn't = would not
shouldn't = should not
couldn't = could not
mustn't = must not

Lesson #30
Question Tags

A *Question tag* is a special construction in English. It is a statement followed by a mini-question. We use question tags to ask for confirmation.
They mean something like: "Is that right?" or "Do you agree?" They are very common in English.

FORMATION OF A QUESTION TAG

Question tags are formed using an auxiliary verb or a form of be (is, am, are) or do (do, does, did) followed by a personal pronoun referring to the subject.

1. If the main clause has an affirmative (positive) sense, then the question tag formed will be negative. A negative tag is always contracted.

   eg:- These mangoes are sweet, aren't they?
   You will come tomorrow, won't you?
   It is raining there, isn't it?

2. If the main clause has a negative sense, then the question tag formed will be positive. A positive tag is not contracted.

   eg:- These mangoes are not sweet, are they?
   You will not come tomorrow, will you?
   It is not raining there, is it?

REPLYING TO A QUESTION TAG

The person to whom you are asking the question would reply to the content of the question and confirms the question with ***yes*** or ***no.***

eg:- These mangoes are sweet, aren't they? = Yes, they are
You will come tomorrow, won't you? = No, I will not

PRACTICE EXERCISES

1. **Fill in the blanks with the correct question tags.**

- They haven't come, ______?
- It didn't sound alright, ______?
- She likes sweets, ______?
- He watches a film every day, ______?
- Some of you open the door, ______?
- Some of you open the door, ______?
- I'm right, _______?
- Julia visited you yesterday, _______?
- The bus stop's over there, _______?
- You won't tell anyone, ________?

Lesson #31

Fillers

Fillers are nothing but a few words or phrases that help us to take some time before uttering the next word/ or sentence (for informal communication).

While speaking, sometimes the accurate word doesn't strike sudden in our mind and sometimes this breaks the fluency in communication.
So, it becomes useful to use fillers so that the fluency is not broken.
Fillers must be avoided in formal communications.

Some Fillers used in communication are:-
"um", **"like"**, **"you know"**, **"it's like"**, **"I mean"**, **"actually"**, **"basically"**, **"well"** etc.

eg:-

- *Umm,* I think you are correct.
- He *is like...* illiterate
- *You know...* I like to travel.
- *Well...* I don't know about Mahesh.
- *I mean...* Ramesh is telling a lie.
- She is, *you know...* she is very intelligent.

NOTE:- Fillers are only to be used during informal communication.
In formal communications, relevant pauses and gestures should be managed.

Lesson #32
Question Structures

In Lesson#30 and Lesson#31, we have gone through the question tags and fillers which make communication easier and fluent.

Now, let's see how we can form questions and present them?

Questions can be of two types

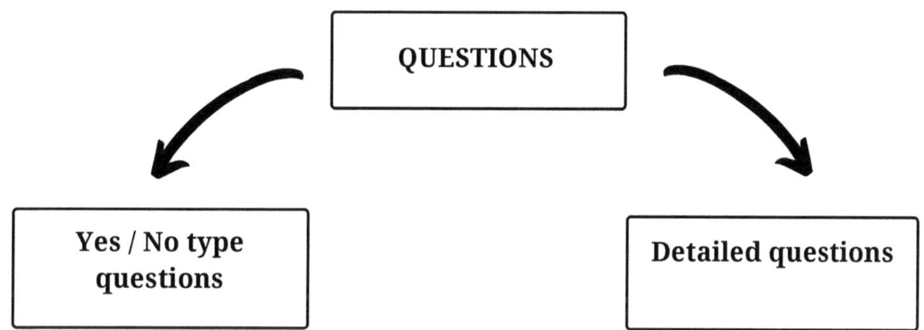

1. **Yes / No type**

   The structure of the Yes or No type questions is:-
   Auxiliary verb + Subject + Verb + Object ?

   eg:- Do you play football?
   Was he going to cinema hall?

2. **Detailed type questions**

   The structure of the Detailed questions is:-
   WH Family + Auxiliary verb + Subject + Verb + Object ?

   eg:- Why do you play football?
   Why Was he going to the cinema hall?
   Where shall we go today?

PRACTICE EXERCISES

1. **Convert the following sentences into questions.**

- The teachers have treated us kindly.
- I could have been studying.
- I went to the store.
- I went to the store.
- I gave him a ride in my car last night.
- He advertised his house for sale.
- I asked the others if they were ready.
- He was stammering.
- I got off the bus.
- Reading is a good habit.
- Ram was with me.
- He will go there himself.
- Aman is my brother.
- Ayush will be 8 months old.
- He reached the office pretty early.
- He can be sent by his father.
- I will come home at Holi.
- Rahul scored 90 out of 100.

Lesson #33
Synonyms & Antonyms

SYNONYMS

Synonyms are words that have the same or very similar meanings.

Words	Synonyms
Amazing	Incredible, Unbelievable, Improbable
Angry	Wrathful, Furious, Enraged
Answer	Reply, Respond,
Ask	Question, Inquire, Query
Beautiful	Gorgeous, Dazzling, Magnificent
Begin	Start, Initiate, Launch
Big	Enormous, Huge
Calm	Quiet, Peaceful
Come	Approach, Arrive
Cry	Weep, Sob, Wail
End	Stop, Finish
Explain	Elaborate, Clarify
Fast	Quick, Rapid
Funny	Humorous, Amusing
Get	Acquire, Obtain
Go	Depart, Recede
Good	Excellent, Marvellous
Idea	Thought, Concept, Notion
Important	Necessary, Vital
Keep	Hold, Maintain, Sustain
Lazy	Idle, Inactive

Words	Synonyms
Love	Like, Admire, Esteem
New	Modern, Current, Recent
Part	Portion, Section, Fragment
Right	Correct, Factual, True
Run	Race, Sprint, Rush
Show	Display, Exhibit

ANTONYMS

Antonyms are words that have the opposite meaning.

Words	Synonyms
Accept	Refuse
Advantage	Disadvantage
Alive	Dead
Ancient	Modern
Answer	Question
Artificial	Natural
Asleep	Awake
Agree	Disagree
All	None
Beginning	Ending
Below	Above
Bent	Straight
Better	Worse
Birth	Death
Bless	Curse
Blunt	Sharp
Blame	Praise
Bitter	Sweet
Borrow	Lend
Break	Repair
Broad	Narrow
Careful	Careless
Calm	Angry
Cheap	Costly
Child	Adult

Words	Synonyms
Clever	Foolish
Combine	Separate
Confident	Timid
Correct	Incorrect
Danger	Safe
Deep	Shallow
Demand	Supply
Expensive	Cheap
Far	Near
Foolish	Clever
Famous	Unknown
First	Last
Freedom	Slavery
Friend	Enemy
Gentle	Harsh
Happy	Sad
Hate	Love
Healthy	Unhealthy
Heavy	Light
Honest	Dishonest
Inferior	Superior
Interior	Exterior
Justice	Injustice
Late	Early
Lazy	Energetic
Little	Big
New	Old
On	In
Open	Close
Out	In
Poor	Rich
Private	Public
Pure	Impure
Scatter	Gather
Sour	Sweet
Sorrow	Joy
Start	End
Strong	Weak

Words	Synonyms
Wet Win Young	Dry Lose Adult

Lesson #34

Phrasal verbs

Phrasal Verbs are usually two-word phrases, consisting of a verb for sure and mostly the other word is a preposition.
Phrasal verbs are used continuously by natives, so they can both help you communicate and improve your vocabulary.

Now, let's see the different phrasal verbs and the way we use them in sentences and communication.

Phrasal verb	Meaning	Meaning
Aim at	Target	The book is ***aimed at*** spoken english.
Ask out	Invite someone for a date	He wanted to ***ask*** her ***out*** but he was feeling shy.
Back up	Make a copy of computer data , support	You should always ***back up*** your important files and data.
Be in	Be at home	I will ***be at*** home
Be snowed under	Have too much work	I am completely ***snowed under*** at work because it is the last month to complete the task.
Be taken aback	Be shocked or surprised	I was ***taken aback*** by his new look.

Blank out	Have a temporary memory loss	I was very nervous in the examination hall that I just **blanked out** and could not answer the questions.
Blow out	Extinguish candles, matches etc.	She ***blew*** the candles ***out***.
Book up	Reserve	The train is fully ***booked up***.
Boss about	Use excessive authority to control people	She ***bosses*** everyone ***about***.
Break down	Start crying	As he lost his toy, he ***broke down*** in tears.
Call off	Cancel	The game was ***called off*** because of heavy rainfall.
Calm down	Stop being angry	It is best to ***calm down*** in adverse circumstances.
Carry on	Continue	You must ***carry on*** with your work.
Carry out	Perform a task	They also ***carry out*** experiments.
Check in	Register on arriving at a hotel or an airport.	Yesterday, they ***checked into*** the Taj Hotel.
Check out	Pay the bill when leaving a hotel	She ***checked out*** and took a cab to the airport.

Come on	Encouragement	***Come on!*** You can do it.
Come up	Appear	I will be late because something has ***come up*** at work.
Come up with	Think of a solution or an excuse	He ***came up with*** a great idea to solve the issue.
Cool down	Become calm , Get cooler	I left the tea for a minute until it had **cooled down** enough to drink.
Cut down	Consume less	We had ***cut down*** our calorie intake.
Cut off	Disconnect	Our electricity has been ***cut off*** for not paying our bill.
Doze off	Fall asleep	He ***dozed off*** while studying.
Dress up	Dress very smartly	She ***dressed up*** as a princess for her birthday party.
Drop out	Quit a course	He ***dropped out*** of college and worked on his startup.
Fall for	Fall in love	Don't ***fall for*** his tricks.
Figure out	Find a solution	The police could not ***figure out*** how the burglars entered the museum.
Fill up	Fill something quickly	I need to fill up with petrol before we go.

Find out	Discover	Let's ***find out*** what's there in the box.
Fix up	Make an arrangement	He ***fixed up*** an appointment with Mr Sharma.
Focus on	Concentrate	You should ***focus on*** your goals to become a successful person in the future.
Get back	Return	We didn't ***get back*** home as it was pouring.
Get in/on	To board a vehicle	He ***gets in*** the car.
Get off/down	To leave a vehicle	He ***gets off*** the bus.
Get out of	To leave for outside	I should ***get out of*** my extra work.
Get together	Meet socially	The two of us ***get together*** after a long time.
Get up	To wake up, To stand up	He ***gets up*** at 7 a.m.
Go through	Read again	You should ***go through*** the book twice.
Grow up	Mature	She ***grew up*** in London..
Hang on	Wait	Could you hang on for a moment till she is free?
Hang out	Spend time socially	She hangs out with her friends every evening.

Hang up	End a phone call	I lost my temper and ***hang up*** on her.
Hit on	Have an idea	I suddenly ***hit on*** the perfect plan for the fest.
Jot down	Make a quick note	I ***jotted down*** her number on a scrap of paper and I can't find it now.
Keep on	Continue	He ***kept on*** trying and completed it successfully.
Lead to	Result in	Poor planning will ***lead to*** difficulty later.
Look back	Think about the past	Adults often ***look back*** on their childhood as a golden age.
Make up for	Compensate	They hurried on to ***make up*** for the lost time.
Mix up	Confuse	He ***mixed up*** the water and the castor oil.
Pick up	Choose	He knelt down to ***pick up*** his hat.
Point out	Make someone aware of something	He was always very keen to ***point out*** my mistakes.
Read out	Read aloud	She read out the names of the candidates who passed the exams.

Run out of	Have none left	I've ***run out of*** patience.
Save up	Save money	You should ***save up*** and get a house.
See off	Say goodbye to someone	Her parents went to the railway station to ***see her off***.
Set off	Start a journey	I ***set off*** for work.
Shut down	Close a business, shop etc. Turn a computer off	He decided to ***shut down*** the shop.
Sit around	Doing nothing	He doesn't like to ***sit around*** and wait for something to happen.
Speak out	Talk openly and freely	***Speak out;*** we can't hear you.

Lesson #35

Communication Dialogues

1. **Informal Greetings**

Gopal :- Hi Deepak, how's it going?
Deepak :- I am doing great. What about you?
Gopal :- Just fine. Where are you going?
Deepak :- To the library. I have got my exams next week and need to study.
Gopal :- Oh I see, Well, I'll see you later then. Good luck.
Deepak :- Thanks. See you later.

2. **What time is it?**

Sam :- What time is it? We're getting late.
Gaurav :- Oh! It is half past nine. We are on time. Don't panic.

3. At a stationery shop?

Mohan :- Hi uncle.
Shopkeeper :- Hi Mohan, how are you doing?
Mohan :- I am doing great. How are you, uncle?
Shopkeeper :- Beta! I am fine. What do you want to buy?
Mohan :- Uncle, I need two packets of biscuits, a bottle of shampoo, and two packets of pasta.
Shopkeeper :- Well, ok. Here is your pasta, biscuits and a shampoo bottle. Anything else?
Mohan :- No uncle. How much is this going to cost me?
Shopkeeper :- It is rupees 210.
Mohan :- ok. But I only have 200. Could I give you the rest 10 rupees a time later?
Shopkeeper :- Yeah, no worries, you can give me that later.

4. Talk between guests and the family members.

Mrs Sharma :- Why are you standing there? Come in, please.
Mrs Sen :- Many thanks for your invitation and warm reception.
Mrs Sharma :- I am really pleased to see you after a long time.
Mr Sen :- We too are much pleased.
Mrs Sharma :- Samir, where are you?
Samir :- Here I am mom.
Mrs Sharma :- Come here and be introduced to our guests.
Samir :- yes mother
Mrs Sharma :- Samir, here is Mr Sen and Mrs Sen
Samir :- Hello, I am Samir Sharma.
Mrs Sen :- Very glad to see you.
Samir :- I am also glad to have you among us.
Mr Sen :- I see, you have a wonderful collection of paintings. These are marvellous.
Samir :- Yeah sir, I like drawing and I have drawn these in my free time
Mr Sen :- Oh, I see, You are a talented artist.
Samir :- Thank you, sir
Mr Sen :- Where is Mr Sharma?
Mrs Sharma :- He is currently in Delhi on an urgent business trip.

5. Talk between two friends

Rajesh :- Hello Sunil, how are you?
Sunil :- I am well, and you?
Rajesh :- I am fine.
Sunil :- So, it is after a long time when we met.
Rajesh :- Indeed it is. By the way, what are you doing now?
Sunil :- I am working as a manager of one of the branches of the State Bank of India. And what do you do?
Rajesh :- I am employed as a teacher in St. Edmund High School in Hyderabad.
Sunil :- I felt quite happy to talk to you after a long time.
Rajesh :- You are right.

6. Talk between a doctor and a patient

Deepak :- I want to meet Dr Gupta
Dr Gupta :- Here I am. What can I do for you?
Deepak :- good morning doctor I have been feeling weak since the last Tuesday.
Dr Gupta :- Do you feel any pain in the body
Deepak :- No I don't but I have a loss of appetite and a general feeling of weakness.
Dr Gupta :- will you take a shirt and coat of a lie down on the coach, please.
Deepak :- Yeah sure.
Dr Gupta :- it seems fine. Is there any vomiting tendency?
Deepak :- not always at times I have a general feeling of nausea.
Dr Gupta :- All right. There is nothing serious. Take this prescription. You will meet me after a week.
Deepak :- Thank you Dr Gupta.

7. **Filing a police report or a diary.**

Rambabu :- Sir, I want to make a diary.
Police Officer :- For what
Rambabu :- Last night a theft has been committed in my house.
Police Officer :- Ok, when did it happen?
Rambabu :- It happened at the midnight sir
Police Officer :- Which things have been stolen?
Rambabu :- Sir cash of three thousand rupees, some jewellery and ornaments.
Police Officer :- Where did you keep all the stolen things?
Rambabu :- I kept the things in an almirah in a room next to my bedroom.
Police Officer :- have you any servant in your house?
Rambabu :- I have a maidservant in my house
Police Officer :- Do you suspect her?
Rambabu :- No she seems to be faithful.
Police Officer :- Do you suspect any other Person
Rambabu :- No I don't suspect anyone
Police Officer :- However I have written your complaint and I am coming after a few minutes you must be at your home and wait for me.
Rambabu :- Thank you, sir. Please come early as possible.

8. **Talk between a receptionist and a person at hotel**

Receptionist :- Good Morning! How can I assist you?
Guest :- Good Morning. I was looking for a room in your hotel. Can you provide me with information regarding that?
Receptionist :- Sure ma'am. We have a room which will cost you INR 1800 per day. You will get complimentary breakfast and dinner.
Guest :- Is the price negotiable?
Receptionist :- If you pay by debit or credit card, you will get a 10% discount.
Guest :- Will I get a discount on online booking?
Receptionist :- Yes sir you will get a 15% discount if you book through our app.
Guest :- So how much do I have to shell out?
Receptionist :- It will cost you around INR 1530 plus taxes per day
Guest :- OK.
Receptionist :- How long are you planning your stay?
Guest :- For a week.
Receptionist :- And when is your expected check-in date?
Guest :- Today.
Receptionist :- Sir you have to pay 2 days in advance at the time of check-in.
Guest :- Why so?
Receptionist :- Sir this is the policy of our hotel and we have to adhere to it.
Guest :- OK, no problem. But before the check-in could you please show me the room.
Receptionist :- Sure, Sir.

9. **Talk between a receptionist and a person at hotel**

Manager :- I need someone to give a vote of thanks in the function today. Everyone is backing out.
Member :- Perhaps I could do it sir
Manager :- Thank you for your offer. But I'm afraid you have a bad cough. That might come in the way of your performance.
Member :- Of course, Sir. But I'll manage
Manager :- Thank you for your spirit. But let's not take a risk. You'll need your voice for next week's culturals

LET'S COMPILE THE THINGS:

- **ASKING PREFERENCES**

  Would you prefer_________? (neutral)
  What do you say about _________? (informal)
  Which appeals more, _____ or ____? (formal)

- **SHOWING PREFERENCES**

  I would prefer _________. (neutral)
  I would go for _________. (informal)
  I generally find _________ more satisfactory. (formal)

- **INVITING SOMEONE**

  I would like to invite you _________ (neutral)
  Why don't you join us for _________? (informal)
  We would be delighted if you could _________. (formal)

- **ACCEPTING INVITATION**

  That'd be very nice. (informal)
  I won't say no. (informal)
  We/I would be delighted to invite you. (formal)

- **DECLINING INVITATION**

  I'm sorry, I can't _________. (informal)
  I won't be here. (informal)
  That's kind of you, but I am unfortunately not able to attend _________. (formal)

- **ASKING FOR HELP**

  Can I help you out with _________? (informal)
  Would you like any help? (formal)

- **ASKING SOMEONE TO SAY SOMETHIMG AGAIN**

  What was that? (informal)
  I am sorry , would you mind repeating the word? (formal)

- **ASKING FOR PERMISSION**

  Do you mind if _________? (neutral)
  Mind if I _________. (informal)
  With your permission, I should like to _________. (formal)

- **GIVING PERMISSION**

  Please don't hesitate. (neutral)
  Go Ahead. (informal)
  Permission is granted _________. (formal)

- **DECLINING PERMISSION**

  I'd like to but I can't _________. (informal)
  I'm afraid, we don't have the authority. (formal)

- **GIVING A REASON**

  The point is _________. (informal)
  The main reason is that _________. (formal)

- **WORDS FOR ENCOURAGING SOMEONE**

  Come on! You can do it! (informal)
  You have our whole-hearted support. (formal)

Lesson #36

Word Bank

ANIMALS

Words	Pronunciation
animal	a - ni - muhl
ant	ant
bat	bat
bear	beuh
bee	bee
bird	buhd
butterfly	buh - tuh - flai
calf	kaaf
camel	ka - muhl
cat	kat
caterpillar	ka - tuh - pi - luh
cockroach	kawck - roche
cow	cow
crab	crab
crocodile	kraw - kuh - dile
deer	dee - uh
dog	dog
donkey	dawnk - kee
duck	duck
eagle	ee - gahl
eel	eel
elephant	eh - luh - funt
fish	fish
fly	fly
fox	fox

Words	Pronunciation
giraffe	juh - raaf
goat	gote
goose	goose
grasshopper	grass - haw - puh
hen	hen
hippopotamus	hip - puh - paw - tuh - muhs
horse	haws
insect	in - sekt
jellyfish	jelly - fish
kangaroo	kang - guh - roo
kitten	ki - tuhn
ladybird	lay - dee - buhd
lamb	lamb
lion	lai - uhn
lizard	li - zuhd
monkey	munk - key
mosquito	maw - skee - toh
moth	moth
mouse	maaws
octopus	okh - toh - puhs
ostrich	ahws - stri - cch
owl	owl
panda	panda
parrot	pae - ruht
peacock	pi - kock
penguin	peng - guin
pig	pihg
scorpion	skaw - pee - uhn
snake	snake
sparrow	spah - row
spider	spai - duh
squirrel	squ - ui - ruhl
swan	swan
tiger	taaih - guh
tortoise	toh - toi - sz
turkey	tuh - kee
whale	whale
wolf	wulf
worm	vuhm
zebra	zeh - brah

PARTS OF BODY

Words	Pronunciation
ankle	ang - kl
arm	aahm
back	back
blood	bluhd
bone	boh - nn
breast	brest
cheek	cheek
chest	chest
chin	ch - in
ear	ee - uh
elbow	el - boh
eye	ai
eyebrow	ai - bra - au
eyelash	ai - lash
eyelid	ai - lihd
face	face
finger	fing - uh
fist	fist
flesh	flesh
foot	fut
forehead	foh -head
hair	hae - uh
hand	hand
head	head
heart	haat
heel	heel
hip	hip
jaw	jaw
kidney	kid - neeh
leg	leg
lips	lips
liver	li - vuh
lung	luhng
mouth	maauth
muscle	muh - sl
nail	nail
neck	neck
nose	nose
organ	aw - gun
rib	rib

Words	Pronunciation
shoulder skeleton skin spine stomach thigh throat thumb toe tongue tooth voice waist wrist	shole - duh skeh - luh - tn skin spine stuh - muk thai thro - oat thum toe tuhng tooth voys vay - st rist
Senses	
feel hear see smell taste touch	feel hee - uh see smell taste tuh - cch
Body postures	
crouch kneel lie lie down sit sit down stand stand up stretch	kraau- ch neel lie lie down sit sit down stand stand up strech

Words	Pronunciation
Describing people	
age	age
beard	beeuhd
complexion	cuhm - plex - uhn
expression	ex - preh - shun
false teeth	fawls teeth
fringe	frinj
freckles	freh - klz
gesture	jes - chuh
glasses	glasses
hairstyle	hair - staa - aail
height	hite
measurement	meh - zhuh - ment
moustache	muh - staash
scar	skaa
smile	smile
spot	spot
tears	tee -ahz
weight	vayt
wrinkles	ring - kl
bald	bald
beautiful	byoo - ti - ful
big	big
blind	blaaih - ind
blonde	blawnd
curly	Kuhl - ee
dark	dark
disabled	dis - ay - bld
dyed	dyed
fair	fay - uh
fat	fat
handsome	han - sum
old	old
overweight	over - vayt
pretty	prih - tee
short	shawt
skinny	skin - ih
slim	slim
small	small
straight	strayt
tall	tall
thin	thin
ugly	uh - glee
young	yung

BUSINESS

Nouns

Words	Pronunciation
accounts	uh - caunt
advertising	ad - vuh - tai - zing
agent	a - gent
brand	bra - and
budget	buh - juht
business	biz - ness
client	claai - ent
commerce	cawh - muhs
company	kuhm - puh - nee
competition	kawm - puh - tu - shn
consumer	kuhn - syoo - muh
corporation	kaw - puh - ray - shn
costs	kawsts
customer	kus - tuh - muh
deal	dee - eel
debt	det
director	duh - rek - tuh
executive	eg - zeh - kyu - tiv
firm	fuhm
management	man - uhj - ment
manager	man - uh - juh
market	maa - kuht
research	re - suhch
marketing	maa - kuh - ting
product	praw - duhkt
profit	praw - fit
promotion	pruh - mo - shun
publicity	pub - lih - city
retail	re - tail
sales	sales
stocks and shares	stocks - and - shae-uhz
supervisor	su - puh - wise - uh
trade	trade
turnover	turn - ovuh

Verbs	
advertise	ad - vuh - tize
buy	baay
employ	em - ploy
expand	ex - pand
improve	im - proov
invest	in - vest

CELEBRATIONS

Nouns

Words	**Pronunciation**
birthday	buhth - day
bride	bride
ceremony	seh - ruh - muh - nee
Christmas	krus - muhs
death	death
engagement	en - gayj - ment
festival	feh - stuh - vl
funeral	fyoo - nuh - ruhl
gift	gift
groom	groom
invitation	in - vi - teh - shun
marriage	ma - ruhj
New Year's Day	nyoo - ee-uhz - day
occasion	uh - keh - zun
party	paa - tee

Words	Pronunciation
procession Valentine's Day wedding ceremony wedding anniversary	pruh - seh - shun Va - luhn - tinez - day weh - ding ce - re - mony weh - ding ani - vuh - suh - ree
Verbs	
bury celebrate fast get married get engaged invite organize wish	buh - ree seh - luh - brayt fast geht ma - ruhd geht en - gayj in - vaaite or - geh - naaiz wish

CLOTHES

Nouns

Words	Pronunciation
belt blouse boots bra button cap cardigan clothes coat collar dress	behlt blaaws boots braa buh - tuhn kap kaah - dee - guhn clothes kote koll - uh dress

Words	Pronunciation
gown	gaaun
fashion	fae - shun
gloves	gluh - uhvz
hat	hat
handkerchief	han - kuh - cheef
high heels	haai heels
jacket	jack - et
jeans	jeens
nightdress	nayt - dres
panties	pan - teez
pocket	pock - et
sandals	sand - uhls
sari	saari
scarf	skaaf
shirt	shuht
shoes	shooz
shoelaces	shoo - lays - es
shorts	shorts
skirt	skuht
sleeve	sleev
slippers	slip - uhz
sneakers	sneek - uhz
suit	soot
sweater	sweh - tuh
tie	taaih
trainers	trayn - uhz
trousers	trau - zuh
T-shirt	T-shirt
turban	tuh - bn
underwear	un - duh - weuh
uniform	uni - form
vest	vest
zip	zip

COLLEGE AND ACADEMICS

Nouns

Words	Pronunciation
art school	aat skoo - ool
arts	aats
assembly	uh - sem - blee
assignment	uh - sine - muhnt
bachelor's degree	ba - chuh - luh's degree
blackboard	black - board
break	break
bully	buli
campus	kamp - uhs
canteen	kan - teen
class	klass
classroom	klass - room
college	kollege
course	kors
coursework	kors - vuhk
desk	desk
degree	deg - ree
department	deh - paaht - ment
diploma	dip - loma
distance	di - stahns
learning	luhn - ing
essay	eh - say
exam	ex - aam
examination	ex - aam - in - eh - shun
faculty	fahk - ul - tih
fieldwork	feehld - vuhk
finals	faai - nuhlz
graduate	grah - ju - ate
graduation	grah - ju - a - shun
honours degree	Aw - nuhs degree
holidays	holi - days
homework	home - vuhk
janitor	ja - ni - tuh
law school	law skool
lecture	lehk - chuh
lecturer	lehk - chuh - rer
lesson	leh - sun
master's degree	mas - tuhz - dig - ree

Words	Pronunciation
medical school	meh - di - kuhl - skool
mistake	mis - tayk
period	pee - ree - uhd
playground	play - graund
private school	praih - vate skool
public school	puhb - lik skool
pupil	pyoo - pl
recess	re - cez
register	reh - jis - tuh
result	reh - zuhl
research	re - surch
school	skool
semester	seh - meh - stuh
social sciences	so - shuhl - sai - uhns
student	stu - dent
student loan	stu - dent - loan
student union	stu - dent - u - nion
syllabus	si - leh - buhs
term	tuhm
tutor	tyoo - tuh
subject	sub - ject
teacher	tee - chuh
textbook	tekst - buk
tutorial	tuh - taw - ri - uhl
undergraduate	un - duh - grah - joo - uht
university	u - ni - vuh - sity
viva	vaih - va
vocational course	voh - kay - shun - ul kors
Verbs	
ask	aask
answer	aan - suh
bully	bu - lee
cheat	cheeht
correct	kuh - ruhkt
enroll	en - roll
fail	fail
graduate	grah - joo - uht
invigilate	in - vih - juh - late
pass	pass

Words	Pronunciation
punish	puh - nish
repeat	re - peat
registe	reh - jis - tuh
revise	re - vaaiz
study	stuh - dee
teach	teach

COOKING AND KITCHEN

Nouns

Words	Pronunciation
barbecue	baa - buh - kyoo
blender	blen - dr
bottle	baw - tuhl
opener	open - er
broiler	broy - luh
chopping	chaw - ping
board	board
coffee maker	kaw - fee - mae - kuh
cook	kook
cooker	kook - uh
corkscrew	kawk - skri - eeu
dish	dish
food	food
processor	praw - seh - suh
fork	fawk
frying pan	fraa - ing - pan

Words	Pronunciation
grater	grai - tuh
grill	grill
kettle	keh - tuhl
knife	naaif
microwave	maai - kruh - vayv
mixing bowl	mix - ing bole
pan	pan
peeler	peel - uh
pot	pot
recipe	reh - sih - pee
saucepan	sauce - pan
sieve	siv
spoon	spoon
toaster	toast - er
Verbs	
bake	bayk
beat	beet
boil	bawyl
bring	bri - ing
chop	chop
cook	kook
fry	fraaih
grill	gri - ill
melt	meh - lt
peel	peel
prepare	pre - peh - uh
roast	row - st
serve	suhv
slice	slaai - s
stir	stir
weigh	wayh

FEELINGS AND QUALITIES

Nouns

Words	Pronunciation
anger	ang - uh
excitement	ex - saayt - mehnt
fear	fee - uh
feeling	feel - ing
feelings	feel - ing - s
guilt	gilt
happiness	ha - pih - nehs
honesty	aw - nuhst - tee
intelligence	in - teh - li - juhns
kindness	kind - nehs
mood	mood
nature	nay - chuh
personality	puh - sun - uh - lee - tee
pride	pra - aihd
quality	kvaw - luh - tee
regret	ruh - gret
relief	ruh - leef
spite	spaait
stupidity	stu - pi - di - ty

Adjectives

Words	Pronunciation
ambitious	am - bi - shi - us
angry	ang - ri
annoyed	uh - noyd
anxious	an - shi - us
ashamed	uh - shaymd
bored	bored
calm	ca - am
cheerful	chee - uh - ful
well-behaved	well - be - haevd
worried	wuh - rid

Words	Pronunciation
Verbs	
become behave calm down enjoy feel grow hurt suffer upset	be - cuhm be - have ca - am daawn en - joy feel grow huht su - fuh up - set

FRIENDS & FAMILY

Nouns

Words	Pronunciation
adult	a - dult
aunt	aant
aunty	aan - tih
baby	baby
bachelor	bach - luh
boy	boy
boyfriend	boy - frend
brother	bruh - thuh
brother-inlaw	bruh - thuh - in - law
child	chaild
couple	kuh - puhl
cousin	kuh - zn
dad	dad
daughter	daw - tuh

Words	Pronunciation
daughter-in-law	daw - tuh -in-law
family	fa - mi - li
father	faa - thuh
father-in-law	faa - thuh - in - law
friend	frend
girl	guh - rl
girlfriend	guh - rl - frend
grandchild	grand - chaaild
granddaughter	grand - daw-tuh
grandfather	grand - faa - thuh
grandma	grand - ma
grandmother	grand - muh - thuh
grandparents	grand - pae - rents
grandson	grand - sun
grown-up	grown - up
husband	hus - band
mother	muh - thuh
mother-in-law	muh - thuh - in-law
neighbour	neih - buh
nephew	neh - phew
nickname	nick - name
niece	nees
orphan	awr - fuhn
parents	pae - rents
relative	ruh - la - tive
sister	sis - tuh
sister-in-law	sis - tuh -in-law
son	sun
son-in-law	sun-in-law
stepbrother	step - bruh - thuh
stepdaughter	step - daw-tuh
stepfather	step - faa - thuh
stepmother	step - muh - thuh
stepsister	step - sis - tuh
stepson	step - sun
surname	suh - name
teenager	teen - ager
twins	twins
uncle	uhn - kl
widow	wi - dow
widower	wi - dow - er
wife	waaif

Words	Pronunciation
Verbs	
adopt	a - dopt
break up	break up
divorce	di - vors
fall out	fall out
foster	fos - tuh
get divorced	get divorced
get married	get married
marry	marry
go out with	go out with
someone	some - one
grow up	grow up
make friends	make friends
make up	make up
Adjective	
dead	dead
divorced	di - vorced
engaged	eng - aged
grown-up	grown-up
married	mah - rid
pregnant	preg - nant
separated	sep - rated
single	sing - uhl

HEALTH

Nouns

Words	Pronunciation
accident	ak - suh - dent
ache	ek
ambulance	am - bu - laens
bandage	band - age
bridge	brij
cancer	can - suh
cold	cold
cough	kuhf
crutch	kruch
dentist	den - tist
diarrhoea	dai - rhea
diet	diet
doctor	dok - tur
first aid kit	fuhst aid kit
germ	juh - rm
health	helth
heart attack	hart - uh - tack
hospital	hos - pih - tuh
illness	ill - ness
injection	in - jek - shun
measles	mee - zlz
medicine	meh - dih - suhn
nurse	nuhs
operation	aw - puh - reh - shun
pain	payn
patient	pay - shnt
pharmacy	faa - muh - see
pill	pill
plaster	plas - tuh
poison	poy - zn
pregnancy	preg - nan - see
prescription	pres - krip - shun
pulse	puhls

Words	Pronunciation
scratch sore throat stomach ache stress tablet temperature thermometer wheelchair x ray	skrach sore throt stuh - muhk ayk stres tab - let tem - pruh - chuh thuh - maw - muh - tuh veel - chay - uh x ray
Verbs	
bleed cough cure cut die faint feel better feel sick itch rest scratch sneeze vomit	bleed kuhf kyor kuht die faynt feel beh - tuh feel sick ich rest skratch sneez vo - mit

HOUSES

Nouns

Words	Pronunciation
Apartment	uh - paat - muhnt
Attic	a - tic
Balcony	baal - kuh - nee
Basement	base - ment
Bathroom	bath - room
Bedroom	bed - room
Building	bil - ding
Ceiling	si - lihng
Chimney	chim - ni
Cottage	cawt - age
Dining room	dai - ning room
Door	dohr
Doorbell	dohr - bell
Doorstep	dohr - step
Entrance	en - trehns
Flat	flat
Floor	flor
Garage	guh - raaj
Garden	gah - den
Gate	gayt
Hall	hall
Kitchen	ki - chen
Landlord	land - lord
Landlady	land - lady
Lavatory	la - vuh - tuh - ree
Lift	lift
Living room	li - ving room
Owner	oh - nuh
Property	pro - puh - tee
Rent	rent
Roof	roof
Room	room
Shutters	shuh - tuhz
Stairs	stay - uhz

Words	Pronunciation
Storey	stoh - ree
Tenant	teh - nant
Wall	wall
Window	win - dow
Yard	yaahdd
Armchair	ahm - cheh - uh
Bed	bed
Bookcase	book - kais
Chair	chey - uh
Cot	cawt
Cupboard	kuh - buhd
Desk	desk
Drawer	draw - uhr
Furniture	fuh - ni - chuh
Lampshade	lamp - shade
Mattress	mah - tres
Shelf	shelf
Sofa	sofa
Stool	stool
Table	teh - buhl
Wardrobe	ward - robe
Appliance	app - li - ahns
Computer	khm - pyu - tuh
Cooker	cook - uh
Dishwasher	dish - wash - uh
Freezer	free - zuh
Fridge	frij
Hairdryer	hay - uh - drai - uh
Heater	heet - uh
Iron	ai - uhn
Ironing board	ai - uhn - ing boad
Kettle	keh - tuhl
Lamp	lamp
Microwave oven	mai - kro - wave oven
Phone	fone
Radio	reh - di - oh
Stereo	steh - ree - oh
Telephone	tele - phone
Television	tele - vi - shun
Vacuum cleaner	vac - uum clean - er
Washing machine	wash - ing machine
Bin	bin
Blanket	blank - et

Words	Pronunciation
Brush	brush
Bucket	buh - keht
Carpet	kar - pet
Clock	klock
Curtain	kuh - tain
Cushion	kuh - shun
Dust	dust
Duster	dust - uh
Key	key
Laundry	laun - drih
Light	light
Lock	lock
Mirror	mih - ruh
Ornament	oh - nah - ment
Pillow	pi - low
Plug	plug
Rubbish	ruh - bish
Rug	rug
Sheet	sheet
Shower	shaau - uh
Soap	sope
Socket	sock - eht
Switch	swich
Tap	tap
Toilet	toi - let
Toothpaste	tooth - payst
Toy	toy
Tray	tray
Vase	vaaz

PROFFESSIONS & CAREERS

Nouns

Words	Pronunciation
Accountant	uh - ka - aaunt
Architect	aar - ki - tekt
Builder	bil - duh
Businessman	biz - nis - man
Businesswoman	biz - nis - wu - man
Carer	ka - uhr - uh
Carpenter	car - pen - tuh
Cashier	cash - i - uh
Chef	shef
Cleaner	cleen - uh
Clerk	cluhk
Cook	cook
Dentist	den - tist
Doctor	dok - tuh
Editor	eh - di - tuh
Eledtrician	e - lek - tri - shi - un
Engineer	en - ji - nee - uh
Farmer	faah - muh
Firefighter	fai - uh - fai - tuh
Goldsmith	gold - smith
Hairdresser	hay - uh - dress - uh
Housewife	haaus - waaif
Journalist	juh - nuh - list
Judge	juhj
Jeweler	joo - uh - lr
Lawyer	law - yuh
Lecturer	lek - chu - ruh
Librarian	laaib - reh - ri - uhn

Words	Pronunciation
Manager	mah - nuh - juh
Mechanic	mek - ah - nik
Miner	miner
Monk	munk
Musician	mew - zi - shian
Nun	nun
Nurse	nurs
Optician	awp - ti - shian
Pinter	paint - uh
Plumber	plum - buh
Police officer	puh - lis - aw - fi - suh
Postman	post -man
Priest	preest
Programmer	pro - gram - uh
Publisher	pub - lish - uh
Receptionist	re - sep - shun - ist
Salesman	sales - man
Saleswoman	sales - wuman
Secretary	sehk - re - tree
Shop assistant	shop - uhs - is - tant
Shopkeeper	shop - keep - uh
Soldier	sol - juh
Surgeon	sur - ji - uhn
Teacher	teach - er
Technician	tehk - ni - shi - un
Vet	vet
Waiter	wayt - uh
Waitress	wayt - ress
Writer	raai - tuh

PERSONAL CARE

Nouns

Words	Pronunciation
bracelet	brace - let
brush	brush
comb	com
cotton	co - tuhn
deodrant	deo - drant
diamond	dai - muhnd
earring	ear - ring
face cream	face creem
gel	gel
hairdryer	hair - dry - er
hairspray	hair - spray
handbag	hand - bag
handkerchief	han - ker - cheef
jewellery	juu - uhl - ri
lipstick	lip - stick
make-up	make - up
mirror	mir - uhr
mouthwash	mouth - wash
nail-paint	nail - paynt
necklace	neck - lace
perfume	puh - fyoom
purse	purs
razor	rae - zuh
ring	ring
shampoo	sham - poo
soap	sop
sponge	sponj
tissue	ti - shu

Words	Pronunciation
toothbrush toothpaste towel wallet watch	tooth - brush tooth - paste towl wo - luht woch
Verbs	
brush crazy comb wear	brush krazi com wee - uh

ROUTINES

Nouns

Words	Pronunciation
chores eat free time habit hobby jogging lifestyle routine sleep	chawz eat free taaim ha - bit hoby jog - ing life - style ru - teen sleep

TIME

Nouns

Words	Pronunciation
time past present future	time past pruh - znt fyu - chuh
Telling a time	
hour minute seconds half an hour quarter past quarter to half past	haur mih - nit se - kehnds haaf an hour qua - tuh past qua - tuh to haaf past
Times of day	
dawn morning noon afternoon evening dusk night summer rainy spring winter autumn	dawn moh - ning noon af - tuh - noon eev - ning dusk night su - muh rainy spring win - tuh au - tuhm

WEATHER

Nouns

Words	Pronunciation
air	a - uh
atmosphere	at - muhs - fee - uh
climate	klai - mayt
cloud	klaa - ud
darkness	dark - ness
drought	drow
flood	fluhd
fog	fog
frost	frost
hail	hail
hailstorm	hail - stomh
lightning	light - ning
monsoon	mon - soon
rain	rain
rainbow	rain - bow
snow	snow
storm	stom
thunder	thun - der
thunderstorm	thun - der - stom
umbrella	um - breh - laa
weather	weh - thuh
wind	wind

9 798885 218580

Printed by Libri Plureos GmbH in Hamburg,
Germany